# Affiliate M............g
# For Beginners

Build Your Own Six Figure Business With
Clickbank Products, Internet Marketing And
Affiliate Links

*(Earn Passive Income And Commissions Fast!!)*

**By Mark Glazer**

Published By **Zoe Lawson**

**Mark Glazer**

*Affiliate Marketing For Beginners: Build Your Own Six Figure Business With Clickbank Products, Internet Marketing And Affiliate Links (Earn Passive Income And Commissions Fast!!)*

ISBN  978-1-77485-467-9

No part of this guidebook shall be reproduced in any form without permission in writing from the publisher except in the case of brief quotations embodied in critical articles or reviews.

Legal & Disclaimer

The information contained in this ebook is not designed to replace or take the place of any form of medicine or professional medical advice. The information in this ebook has been provided for educational & entertainment purposes only.

The information contained in this book has been compiled from sources deemed reliable, and it is accurate to the best of the Author's knowledge; however, the Author cannot guarantee its accuracy and validity and cannot be held liable for any errors or omissions. Changes are periodically made to this book. You must consult your doctor or get professional medical advice before using any of the suggested remedies, techniques, or information in this book.

Upon using the information contained in this book, you agree to hold harmless the Author from and against any damages, costs, and expenses, including any legal fees potentially resulting from the application of any of the information provided by this guide. This disclaimer applies to any damages or injury caused by the use and application, whether directly or indirectly, of any advice or information presented, whether for breach of contract, tort, negligence, personal injury, criminal intent, or under any other cause of action.

You agree to accept all risks of using the information presented inside this book. You need to consult a professional medical practitioner in order to ensure you are both able and healthy enough to participate in this program.

# Table of Contents

# Chapter 1: What Is Affiliate Marketing?

Affiliate marketing is a system that allows affiliates to earn money for the commission of the agreed-upon objective of marketing. Typically, affiliates market products and services of a third party. In addition, they receive a fee for each client they sign up. This arrangement of economics has been in place for as long as companies existed however, it became more evident with the advent that of internet. There are numerous affiliate marketers earning between around six and seven figures. The best part about affiliate marketing is the fact that you have virtually no obstacles to be overcome. All you need to have is an Internet connection and you're good to go.

The majority of people who are in a monotonous job in the corporate world and wish to be free of the stress could do well entering Affiliate marketing. As an affiliate marketing professional, you may even be able to work at your own home. Your earning potential is governed by the level of your hunger to succeed. The more hungry you are, the more effort you'll be putting in and the more money flows into your pocket however, if you're lazy, you will earn very little and , in some cases or none even. The fact that affiliate marketing can provide the freedom to work from home doesn't mean that money will be deposited into your account.

There's a lot to be accomplished, especially in the beginning stages before you are able to set up systems to help make the work simpler. The world that is affiliate marketing constantly changing and affiliate marketers is constantly reinventing themselves to ensure they don't fall behind their competitors.

Advertising is a frequent subject in the world of affiliate marketing. In addition to choosing a lucrative product the methods you use to advertise are a major factor in determining the success of your affiliate marketing campaign overall. A few of the most well-known advertising strategies include display advertisements and social media advertising and video advertising, email marketing and blogging.

Many businesses have adopted affiliate marketing, since it's one of the most effective ways to boost business revenues and brand awareness.

As an affiliate marketer there are a few things that you should be paying attention to in order to avoid being at risk of harming your efforts. Two of the most crucial factors you should consider are the product and merchants. Working with transparent merchants can ensure that your hard-earned money doesn't end up in the trash.

Affiliate marketing is among the most effective ways to get away from the hustle, make time to do important things (and people) that you are passionate about and, perhaps most important achieve financial freedom.

1.1 What is Affiliate Marketing? How does it Do Its Work?

To comprehend how affiliate marketing functions it is first necessary be aware of the principal players. The more knowledge you gain regarding these key players, the better your chances to reach your goals.

Brands: These are businesses or individuals who control the service or product. The industries are as diverse as you can imagine, industries, retail travel, financial services online shopping, etc. Affiliate marketers who earn their most cash are associated with brands. They've been in business for a while and are aware of the workings and pitfalls of the marketplace and the brands count on them to deliver a high return on investment. If you're just beginning to get into affiliate marketing, it is best to avoid brands and partner with affiliate networks.

Affiliates: The affiliate is the partner in marketing of different brands. As an affiliate marketing professional, you are expected to attract more customers to the product you promote and receive a payment as per the contract. The good thing with the affiliate market is it is possible to begin with only a few resources. In the case of example, have a blog, it's sufficient for you to write reviews, publish on social media and even direct your targeted viewers to affiliate hyperlinks.

Affiliate marketing is also an expensive endeavor, as it is possible that you will require a large budget to buy advertising space and traffic. If you've got the funds and are adept in maximizing your campaigns, this combination will yield you huge profit. Affiliate networks: An affiliate network brings together every brand that is interested in having their products and services marketed. Then, affiliate marketers are able to join these affiliate networks to ensure that they can advertise the program which they feel adequately equipped to advertise. Affiliate marketers who are new to the field should join affiliate networks in order they be able to access the many affiliate programs, and have a an opportunity to determine which they're best at. Affiliate networks also manage the monitoring, reporting, and payment, which means that affiliate marketers will not have difficulty claiming their earnings since there's a proven way of working.

The affiliate marketer is a person who promotes the services or products of a company with the goal of growing sales, and is the compensation they agreed to as per their contract in the affiliation network, or the brand.

## 1.2 How do Affiliate Marketers Earn Money?

Given the variety of merchandise and services that are promoted There will be a variety of metrics for paying affiliate marketers. The most important thing is that the affiliate marketer be aware of what is expected by them and to align themselves in the direction of the organization that promises highest benefits. For instance, if , for example, you have a website for real estate it makes more sense financially to join the affiliate programs that is looking for emails of prospective customers in the real estate industry rather than joining one that targets hosting customers for your website. Here are the typical indicators by which affiliate marketers are paid.

Payment per sales: In this instance an affiliate marketer gets the commission for every customer who purchases the product.

Affiliate networks are of companies seeking to increase their sales. If you've got a well-established blog, you'll have an advantage, and you can suggest products that appeal with your target audience. In turn, you'll notice your commissions increasing. You could also participate in buying media and target your traffic in order that they can become customers. Make sure that you're careful and slow, instead of being a flimsy. Inexperienced mistakes can result in a huge loss.

Pay per Click: Not every business is seeking to make a sale. There are some businesses that want to increase their reach. They are willing to hire an affiliate marketing company to drive targeted traffic to their site. So, for each click you make to their site the seller will happily pay you a percentage. In some way affiliate marketers, in particular novices, may be tempted to profit from the situation and use fraudulent clicks to increase their commissions. This nearly always leads to a disastrous end for the affiliates. Be honest in your efforts to earn a profit. As an affiliate marketing professional, you will only be successful if the brand or merchant succeeds.

If you're not a good affiliate then you're contributing to the decline of the brand and if you are successful it means one less employer from the market. It's never a good thing.

Payment per Lead: Data is among the most valuable components of successful companies as both businesses and marketers are aware of this. They're willing to hire affiliates to gather data about their clients. The most valuable information is an email address. There are numerous affiliate programs that pay marketers for each email belonging to an audience they recruit.

The majority of affiliate networks and merchants offer commissions both weekly and also monthly. There are some restrictions for novices, but when they make a significant amount, the limitations are removed. The location of your home and the affiliate network or the merchant of your choice There are a variety of ways in which the affiliate marketer earns commissions. These include check, bank transfer and payment platforms such as PayPal as well as Paxum.

1.3 Why Should You Be an Affiliate Marketer?

Many people working in corporate positions are caught in a race. They have almost little time for their own needs. One of the biggest benefits of becoming an affiliate marketing professional is that you're now at liberty to work on your own conditions. If you're sick you are able to rest and then work the next day. In contrast, if you're enthusiastic, you could put all your energy towards marketing to increase your income. In the workplace you can do as much as you can however, your pay remains the same, while your employer reaps the benefits of your efforts. Here are a few of the many other benefits of working as an affiliate marketer can be an awesome thing.

* It's a broad billion-dollar business

Consider any niche or product that you are interested in, and there is likely to be an affiliate program that is geared towards it. It is more effective through promoting services and goods which you're interested in. If you join any affiliate program, you'll have the chance to choose the program you prefer from a range of offerings. This means that you're earning money while promoting goods that you're passionate about.

* Low-cost

Most of the time, when people decide to quit their corporate jobs and pursue financial independence Most of the time they want to establish their own company. But , setting up and running a profitable company is not something that is easy, since it requires a lot of capital which could easily send you to financial debt. The reality that more than 80percent of businesses fail in the first five years of their existence isn't any more attractive. However, when you're looking at the affiliate market, you don't require anything to start. In fact, with the internet and a functioning social media profile and you'll be on your way to earning your first payment in less than a week.

Expertise is not an absolute requirement Consider becoming surgeon. You must attend school and be certified prior to being able to perform. If you were caught operating on the brain of someone else without having a license, it could be a felony you think? In reality, these rules are fantastic. But in the case of affiliate marketing, results are all that is important. There is a chance that you aren't proficient in marketing a specific product however in the event that you're making an effort to reach your goals in marketing, then you're good enough. You'll be amazed that many profitable affiliate marketing experts have experience in completely different areas.

* Passive income

If you're an accountant at a large pharmaceutical company, you have to be on time to work in order in order to earn a pay. If you aren't at work, then you probably won't earn the amount. When you consider affiliate marketing, it's the perfect chance to earn money while sleeping. However, this will not be done by itself. It is necessary to do massive effort in the beginning to be in a position to earn income passively. For instance, if you run a blog, you need create quality content to ensure that search engines keep driving visitors to your blog and your visitors will respond to your different calls to Action. This way you'll earn in a passive way. This is why there are many affiliate marketers able to travel around all over the world and reside in exotic locales. They may be on the road but they're also making money, so it's not over.

* You can become a thought leader

People trust people who show the ability. If you've been promoting products or services for some time and you've gained more information about the product or service, and that will be evident the message you use to market. If you do you're able to become a thought-leader, and people will look at you for advice on the areas in which the product or service you are marketing is concerned. Being a thought-leader increases your earnings potential since you're in an position to influence the masses, and you also have the option of having higher prices that are higher than average. But you also have to ensure to not abuse the power of your position, otherwise people can be averse to your ideas.

1.4 How to Be an Affiliate Marketer that is Profitable

Many people believe that simply having a

large advertising budget, they're surely going to succeed with affiliate marketing. A great budget and even choosing great programs is good but it's not the end all that affiliate marketing has to offer. There are a variety of factors that you need to think about in order to be a successful affiliate marketer.

* Learn to become specialized

One of the biggest errors that affiliate marketers make is chewing more than they can swallow. The fact that affiliate networks are brimming with of affiliate programs does not necessarily mean that you're free to endorse each and every one of them. They are mostly different for the purpose of giving you the option to choose from a variety of. Therefore, make sure that you're promoting only just a handful of products focused on your area of expertise. If you promote more than one program and products, you're likely to get overwhelmed and lose interest. Additionally, you may be wasting a lot of cash and time. However, if you focus on specific areas and are in the position to increase your earningsand be a thought-leader.

* Make use of multiple traffic sources

Certain affiliate marketers appear to have a preconceived notion about which sources of traffic are the most effective. Perhaps they had successfully a campaign using native ads, and then developed an affinity for native ads, and so on they will always choose native ads in all their campaigns. As an affiliate marketing professional, you need to be a bit adventurous and be able to test the effectiveness of different traffic sources. Sure, you'll lose money, but at the end of the day you'll gain a lot of knowledge of what kinds of traffic sources work most effective for different deals.

* Track your affiliate campaign

If you're not careful If you're not careful, you can lose lots of money in the event of engaging in buying media. Do not just click your affiliate link on the table and hope that commissions will begin to roll into. It is important to monitor the performance of your campaign to ensure that there are no issues or if you discover one, don't waste time in repairing it.

* Research
The common sense says that you have the
highest chance of earning money when you
market products that are that is in high
demand. But you'll only determine the
success of a product through studies. Some
marketers rush into advertising new products
just to take losses. Make sure you are
engaged in research to increase your profits.


* Keep an eye out
The trends in marketing of the 2000s' early
years are not the same as trends in marketing
in the present. The only constant in this world
is the constant changes. In the field that is
affiliate marketing it is imperative to keep an
eye on evolving trends and be able to change,
or you'll be left behind by your competitors. It
is not a good idea to be in a position where
you have to make changes. You must be
aware of shifts and be more flexible. This will
ensure that you're constantly ahead of the
curve. It also ensures that you're always
operating profitable campaigns.

* Be innovative

While it is crucial to keep up to date with current trends in marketing but it's equally essential to be creative. When we speak of creativity We don't mean to suggest that you create the next successful commercial computer. However, creativity implies that you must present your message to customers from an innovative viewpoint. People are very open to new ideas. Creative messages trigger certain emotions in your intended audience , and increases the chance of them becoming customers.

* Choose the appropriate merchant

It is only possible to be successful at affiliate marketing if you work with a reliable merchant or affiliate network. You'll be shocked by the frauds of different affiliate networks and brands. If you fall into trap of a fraudulent merchant all your hard work is ruined and you will not receive any compensation. Therefore, make sure you conduct some investigation before you choose to partner with any particular merchant or network. With the advent online, it's quite easy to find out about companies, thanks to reviews websites. If a business or affiliate network had a scam on someone before there is a good chance that they were upset that they decided to warn to others in the same situation by writing reviews that were negative. It is best to avoid a company or an affiliate program that's garnered numerous negative reviews.

* Make use of tools

There have been significant advances in the field of technology. There are tools that can aid us in carrying out various tasks across all aspects of our lives. In the case of affiliate marketing, you can find a variety of tools, both free and paid which make our job simpler. Make sure you're using these tools to reduce your work load and increase the amount of money you earn.

# Chapter 2: Keyword Research

The quality guidelines are then laid out. Webmasters must follow these to maintain a steady rank. The next step involves a comprehensive description of the needed modifications to a site that will boost the rank numerous times over. These are known as on-page SEO strategies. Based on these helpful guidelines the structured data are satisfied with the dedication of a large number of people and also boost the rank of a site. In addition, the Off-Page SEO is explained in great detail since this isn't to be omitted from the search engine optimization process not anymore.

Keyword research

Keyword research is an essential role in optimizing search engines. Without this, the performance of a site is at risk of failure. Keywords are the words that both users and webmasters are able to identify with an Internet presence. They must be selected carefully. Additionally, web designers slide in the shoes of site visitors when they conduct keyword research. They search for keywords and phrases that people enter into search engines. Then , they position them in a smart way on their website to make sure they rank as high as they can in natural (unpaid) results of searches. The problem is to choose the most relevant keywords that are well-liked by users but stand out from competitors.

Keywords: Types

There are many kinds of keywords. In terms of the intent of the user Keywords can be classified into three distinct groups. These include navigation, informative and commercial keywords.

Commercial keywords are used by people who have the intention of purchasing. An example could be "Buying a travel Guide in the USA". People who market the item they are searching for must select the right keywords and ensure that they clearly communicate your intention to buy.

If you search for "Travel Tips USA", but users who type these keywords have the goal of getting free travel advice. Therefore, the primary goal of this particular user is not to access the website of a travel guide paid for. However, companies that offer articles with no cost tips on traveling in the USA and wish to promote your travel information at end of the article can make use of this keyword. People searching for information about particular topics are able to use informational keywords. The query: "How big is the Eiffel Tower?" is a classic example of using useful keywords. These kinds of questions are great to use for Voice SEO. Webmasters who make use of these terms will not discover any users that have an intention to buy.

Head tail or short keywords comprise only one word. Although this keyword species is not a specific species, it spans the entire variety. Mid tail keywords typically comprise two to three words and are the middle between the general short tail keywords and the specifically long tail terms.

Long tail keywords typically contain more than four words. It is a distinct kind of keyword that gets more precise due by the inclusion of more keywords.

A good example of a shorter or head tail keyword could be "bread". The mid tail extension of a keyword may mean "bake bread". The long tail extension could consist of "bake bread in the kitchen".

Finding the best keywords to optimize your search engine

The term "keyword research" in search engine optimization is the searching for a suitable keyword for a site. The users use the chosen keyword to search for a specific webpage through the Internet. So, the choice that the keywords are used for plays a major part. But, it should not just match the website's content, but also be searched by the targeted audience. The term "keyword" does not mean only one word, but is also the text element that is either within the text or describes the content of the text in an appropriate keyword. In this way, keywords are constructed from a variety of phrases and numbers. They represent words, about which a piece of text is discovered most often through Google as well as other search engines. The most difficult part for webmasters is their ability to position themselves within their intended audience. In the real world, it usually occurs that websites are designed for inappropriate keywords since the audience is using completely different names than the site operator. The purpose of keyword research is to identify the keywords most of users of the targeted group are searching for.

The difference between keywords that are good and bad

Before the steps to conduct a successful keyword search is addressed and the difference between bad and good keywords is established.

An online retailer that sells outerwear like T-shirts and jackets as well as pullovers will probably initially choose the phrase "outerwear" This is in theory perfectly accurate but is actually less popular with the person searching. The issue is whether the audience is actually searching at "outerwear". The answer is no. The term "outerwear" is one of the Head Tail Keyword, which isn't commercially relevant. Even if it does have a large quantity of searches, the amount connected would remain very small due to the fact that this keyword is not accurate. The words "T-shirt" as well as "jacket" do not provide an appropriate alternative, since they don't indicate which audience the users are looking for, as they aren't commercial keywords. If people want to purchase something and are looking for a jacket, they'll use the search term "buy jacket" (commercial keywords). Online sellers who rank their shops for the phrase "jacket" will not reach their target audience directly. Keyword research seeks to formulate a precise formula and a precise alignment of the keywords.

The general rule is: "The more general a keyword is, the higher the number of relevant pages Google will locate". In the same way this creates huge competition. This means that the likelihood of being on the top spot, having has only ranked his store following the keyword "jacket" decreases significantly. Thus, a keyword that describes the specific offerings of the site in the most exact manner feasible, is the primary objective. But, it must be a commercial one. So entrepreneurs can reach their target group with much less effort.

Keyword species that are recommended for

To find the most appropriate keywords, a thorough understanding of the proper keywords is essential. In the past it was the case that long tail keywords dominated SEO. This is due in part to the fact that there are few competition. The reason is that website owners are able to quickly rise to the top of search results. But the issue with long tail keywords is in the volume of their searches. A search number of 100 isn't enough to ensure success for an online site. This is why the optimization of similar long tail terms and related textual content is done by using various keywords. It is therefore not recommended that a web page has five distinct web pages that share similar content, but they are optimized for various Long Tail keywords. This will increase the number of search queries. But, this method has not been successful. Google is now very clever and has a good sense of these techniques. This method ended in the last few days with the known as Panda Update. Because of this, websites operators can only rank as one long tail keyword. This decreases the volume of searches. The following summary provides a summary of the negatives of long tail keywords.

The latest updates block Google indexing multiple pages related to the same subject.

The volume of search results is very small.

Contributions of poor quality can affect negatively the credibility of the website.

Due to the disadvantages listed above, it's worth switching in the direction of Mid Tail Keywords. Even if they're highly popular, but with well-chosen choice and consistent content marketing they could quickly propel an online site to the top of the list.

But, competitiveness is highest for keyword phrases that are short. Webmasters can reach the greatest amount of people using this kind of keyword. However, experience has shown that shorter tail keywords aren't the most effective selection. So, the Mid Tail Keywords are best suited. They are not as competitive. This is due to the fact that they're not as broad as keywords with a short tail. Furthermore, they boost the likelihood of a financial statement to be more reliable.

A thorough keyword study saves webmasters not just time but also money. The right keyword is essential to making money. Keywords that are not appropriate and are not compatible with the website content don't provide any added value to the person searching. Additionally, webmasters who conduct a thorough search engine optimization can identify keywords that their competitors do not employ. This way webmasters can benefit from advantage of competitive competitivity. The most appropriate methods and procedures for conducting keyword search

The next keyword search can be performed using Google. Webmasters do not require equipment that costs money to perform this guide. The keyword research is provided free of cost.

Keyword brainstorming

Find the keywords that correspond to the site in question

The keyword is covered by a cloud, containing other words

If the keyword in question would be "baking bread" other phrases like gluten-free whole meal bread, sunflower flour, or baguette may be used in conjunction with the main key word.

In order to comprehend and apply these techniques, the methods discussed are implemented with the help of the word "baking bread" as an illustration.

Keyword Input in an appropriate keyword tool

These guidelines are for the successful search for keywords, which is done using Google. It is possible to use the Google Keyword Planner will help. Webmasters may also make use of other keyword toolsthat they can access for free. Once the tool has been chosen, the keyword is input into the tool you have selected. People who wish to do the research using AdWords will require an account with a Google account. Webmasters simply type in their principal keyword into the Keyword Planner tool, under "Search to find new keyword phrases with an expression or a website page, and an appropriate category". If you click Ideas Retrieve the various keywords are shown.

Sorting the keyword list by search according to the volume of searches

Users get a variety of keywords which are relevant to the main keyword. By clicking on the area titled "Average monthly search queries" webmasters can sort them in a range of sizes from small to large. Keywords that have the most search volume are at the top of the list. In the final or on the pages with the most results in this listing, keyword that have little search volume are highlighted. Most of the time, these are lengthy tail keyword. Middle ranks can be crucial for webmasters as the majority of mid-tail keywords are found there. Based on this advertisement webmasters pick a keyword which best fits what they are putting on their internet presence. It is recommended that you check out the column that is titled "Competition" as well as look at the pages that are climbing to find the mid-tail keywords. However, since Google Keyword Planner is an AdWords tool, competition is not referring only to the presentation of results from search and general advertisements. This is why webmasters should not ignore the growing web pages for the relevant keyword.

Competitive intelligence

This is the stage where webmasters look at their competitors using the keyword. There are a variety of indicators to determine this. The competition could serve as a sign of how strong the competition is, as well as an indication of an indication of the "interrupted offer". The more expensive the bid is, the greater the competition. However, website developers should not solely rely on this data. This is due to the fact that a specific keyword is very expensive to show and has a huge recognition, yet isn't highly effective in organic results. To find out the extent of competition the chosen keyword is it is worthwhile to apply the following strategies.

Enter the URL as well as your domain's metrics as well as an examination of the backlinks.

Control of Optimization of the ON-Page

Find the appropriate search results for the page with questions or on forums.

Examine the quality of content more carefully

To better comprehend and implement these methods the methods described are executed by using the instance key word "baking bread".

The input of URL as well as the domain metrics, as in addition to a look-up of backlinks

For this webmasters employ a software that provides them with vital metrics. The free tool known as "SEO Toolbar" by the developer MOZ could be useful. It needs to be installed. After the setup is successful, the toolbar, input of keywords occurs on Google. From the present results the toolbar that includes all the metrics of the relevant page and domain is now displayed without effort. Webmasters are particularly interested by the URL Rating value as well as Backlinks / Linking Domains to Websites Domain Rating, Backlinks/Linking Domains to the Full Page. The first step is to analyze the strength to determine the URL rating. This indicates the quality of a particular page. In this instance it is evident that the majority of results are lower than 20. In the end, this implies that competition is within the lower part of the range. Webmasters must not overlook the details on how the website is connected. This is why identifying the origin for the link back is crucial. To accomplish this it is necessary to use a back Link Checker. If you don't possess a tool that is able to display backlinks for a domain could use a tool that is free. If you're looking at the back link of a website that is first ranked, experts recommend you to take into consideration the following points. Based on the rating of the domain webmasters can determine that the most powerful domains are linked directly to the page. Most of the time they are relevant websites. For instance the overview of link types illustrates that, from the total of 41 links only one is labeled "NoFollow". So, almost all backlinks are high-quality. Google places a high value on the content that is presented. The website is in first spot, provides users with an informative content in which they can also get general information regarding the subject of "baking bread". In addition, the metrics for the domains in question are evaluated. If the majority of them have a domain score of 50 or more and only hundreds or thousands of backlinks, webmasters need to recognize that they are unable to be competitive with other websites by having difficulties in this particular keyword.

Control of the OnPage Optimization

Because ON-Page Optimization is an essential element of optimizing search engines Many pages which are not optimized indicate the fact that they have a low level of competition. Through the ON-Page Optimized Control, webmasters can take an in-depth look at results of their searches. The control checks whether the keyword appears within the tag titles. Most entries include the phrase "buy foods supplements". To discover the root of this webmasters must nevertheless be sure to look over the pages. Some important tips for optimizing are given, such as:

Keyword placement in H1 and H2 headings.

Keywords are placed in the relevant URL

Webmasters can choose to visit the website and then manually run the ON-Page Optimization checks or utilize OneProSEO's SEO free Check Tool. This controls on-page optimization. If the keyword is visible in the URL and also in the various H1 headings, excluding the H2 headings this is not a sign that the page has been optimized poorly. Webmasters need to take this action to ensure that they control the top 10 websites. If they spot some or two websites which aren't optimized, they should take this as an indication of a term that has no competition.

Look up the relevant results from the search results on pages with questions or on forums.

For certain keywords, queries from forums or question-answer sites like "gutefrage.net" may also be listed in the top 10. This is a sign of how poorly the competitor's site has been optimized with respect to this particular keyword.

Examine the content's quality more carefully.

The process of ensuring quality of content is the most significant aspect of conducting keyword research. Webmasters look closely at the content of individual pages. If they see a lot of tinny information or dull and too brief articles about "buying diet supplements" This is evidence of low competition. But, if the content about this subject are primarily long and detailed the keyword is an extremely popular keyword. Therefore, it's worth looking for a more suitable keyword. The profile previously mentioned could be a valuable assistance.

The keyword planner of Google

Users searching for keywords within the Google Keyword Planner now find the exact number of keywords as well as the search volume that corresponds to them in the appropriate column. The Google Keyword

Planner allows its users to monitor the exact volume of search. However, they must to be willing to face some hurdles.

The first step is to choose the option "Determine the new keyword". They then conduct a normal search for a key word.

Webmasters need to ensure that they have chosen the correct region Germany. The default setting is always referring towards the USA. This is why it is crucial to be aware of this setting. When you click on the target region and then the language, the user can choose to use an German version.

The keyword planner is now showing the list of keywords, along with the volume of searches and the keywords. It offers useful suggestions for keywords webmasters may utilize. Furthermore, users are provided with information about the keywords in the ads of their rivals. But, they shouldn't use them all at once in any way. An in-depth explanation on this subject is provided on the next pages.

Make use of Wikipedia as a model for appropriate keywords

Not only forums, too Wikipedia will assist webmasters in their research on keywords. In this massive online encyclopedia, a lot of people are making an effort of categorizing articles on various topics into the appropriate categories. All webmasters must do is visit"wikpedia.de," or the "wikpedia.de" site and type the term they wish to search for using the search bar on the top of the page. For optimizing search engines this table of content is especially informative as it provides important suggestions.

Similar searches to Google

Webmasters could, for example search for "search engine optimization" on Google and then scroll down to the very bottom on the webpage. Then, you'll see "relatives searches". This function allows web designers who are motivated can easily and quickly discover mid-tail keywords that can be directly linked to a larger short tail keyword, and therefore could be ideal as their primary keyword.

# Chapter 3: List Of The 20+ Top Affiliate Marketing Niches

## 1. Golf

This should come as no surprise for someone who has been playing the affiliate marketing industry for more than a couple of months however, golf is one of those extremely profitable markets (you will see that the majority of the premium markets are lucrative niche affiliate markets).

In fact, the world golf industry is worth $ 12.55 billion per year. Every year.

The average golfer invests PS 1414 ($ 275) per month, or PS 2,568 ($3,305) each year for his pastime.

While it could appear to be an exclusive pastime but it is enjoyed by everyone from all kinds of backgrounds.

And all of them share one most commonality they love spending whatever they can afford to enhance their performance.

It's true that golf is an extremely competitive field, however I was able to locate 149,000 words with the KD being less than 20 Ahrefs and it is one of the most lucrative niches to affiliate market in 2021.

It's also quite easy to learn about free training and tips. The demand for technical information is high and a lot of websites do not have a lot of success.

2. Home security

I've never considered security for my home that seriously prior to recently. This changed after my home was robbed just more than two years in the past. The possibility of having your home smashed into is an extremely difficult thing to experience.

Security at home was my top priority because my friend was worried about sleeping through the midnight.

The items I've invested in include brand new internal and external locks windows security locks, Wi-Fi cameras, exterior motion sensor lighting, and an alarm system for my home that is monitored that has multiple sensors within the house.

In essence I dropped the most important part of the wing to ensure she was safe and secure. This is one of the aspects that makes affiliate marketing such great niches: the feeling of urgency. Within the US, 1.24 million households are divided each year. Therefore, this is a very focused group that is in need of your assistance.

3. Online dating

It's fascinating how the world of online dating has evolved over the past two decades. There's a market for affiliate marketing that's been in existence since the beginning.

There was a time when those who were able to find a partner via an online dating site was considered to be somewhat ... and ... odd.

Things have changed but online dating isn't only acceptable anymore It's trendy!

What does the Dating Industry really worth? According to the latest estimates, it could reach $2 billion annually with an annual increase of six percent in the near future. This data also indicates that at the very least, 24% of individuals have used or previously used online dating sites previously.

The reason this business has been so successful is due to the fact that no matter what people think, humans are social creatures. We desire to join a tribe and eventually form our own tribe when we reach. The process of helping single women and men reach their goals is one of the most lucrative areas to work with If you are familiar with the most effective programs that are able to be paid for.

4. Travel

There's a vast old world around and the abundance of flights at a reasonable price means that you can travel to even the most remote coastlines without having to be a lottery winner. You may be forced to fly economy class and sacrifice the comfort that comes with business classes, however it's just a tiny cost to pay.

The number of people who travel to and from work is higher than any time in time. This is not good news for governments that are afraid of the spread of pandemics. However, it's a great information for travel companies that is responsible for the estimated amount of 7 trillion dollars (yes there's the letter "t") each year.

It's also one of the most lucrative affiliate niches available and there's a wide array of profitable programs available to assist you with this.

Travel is a broad range of niches and sub-niches that range from standard hotels and flights to city excursions and luggage, insurance as well as clothing. Therefore, you don't need to adopt the same strategy that many members do. Try to find low-cost flight tickets and hotel reservations.

5. Gaming

It's good to know that I constructed my very first computer to enjoy X-Wing in the computer ... in MS-DOS. You're not old! Gaming was always an integral aspect of my life, and it was fascinating to observe how it evolved through each decade.

The audience for gaming has increased to include not just consoles, but even mobiles. Mobile devices are a big part of the world of networks. Around 200 million people play games with video within North America alone, but it's just a small fraction of the population as compared with the 2.5 billion people across the globe.

Gaming is a specialized field similar to golf in the sense that gamers are happy to shell out hundreds of dollars for a new GPU as well as a gaming desk. Then repeat the process each year.

There's an almost luxury market that is in constant demand in this market. The gaming industry is one of the most popular niches for affiliate marketing. But I was found 25,919 keywords that have an average KD of less than 20. There are many gaming niches I could use and there is an growing demand for this niche.

6. Home Decor

The home decor industry is among those niches that are evergreen and worth taking a close glance. Why?

The reason is that homeowners decorate their homes to sell or remodel a home or apartment they've recently purchased. It is typical for people to spend between $ 500 to 5000 on renovating or decorating every space in their house.

What do you think about recessions?

It's exactly the same thing in a smaller extent - walls must paint, couches repaired and so on. But , homeowners will wish to do this at a cost that is affordable in a downturn, and that's an industry in and of itself (but I also like the luxury market too).

The affiliate niche has agreements that offer between 100 to $200 per sale, based on the category of product. Really.

7. Financial

We actually refer to the financial industry as profitable because it's naturally occurring.

We've also added it to this list since the majority of affiliate marketers who are new aren't interested in it as they think it's a saturated segment. It's competitive, but much simpler than, for instance making money by selling adult-oriented content.

In our article about successful Affiliate Marketing Sites we will look at several examples of affiliate businesses earning a significant profit in this area. You're evidence that you need to have a unique viewpoint and are prepared to do your best.

In other words it is that people are getting into more debt than they have ever before. There is a massive market for the services and products that we've found for you. If you're able to succeed, you'll be one of the most lucrative affiliate marketing niches. However, you must be an experienced marketer in this field.

8. Cruises

Growing up, I believed that only rich people would take cruises. Perhaps that was once the case, but not any more.

Here's a nutshell around the area of 26 million passengers go to cruises each year. These same folks living in the area will shell out $3600 on their sea-based vacations. All of this adds up to an industry worth approximately $125 billion per year.

All walks of life travel on cruises There are even cruises catering for everyone from singles to rock enthusiasts. One suggestion is to identify the sub-niche and/or focus on the thousands of informative keywords with poor KD scores. It could be a lucrative market if you choose the proper approach.

9. Fitness

Another one of those evergreen niches you can be certain will be in the next 50 years. It's because the fitness market has been in existence for, let's say for a little over four hundred years.

The ancient empires required that young men train physically, typically for battle however, you must also take a look at the first Olympics around 2700 years ago.

Whatever the case, the idea we're trying to convey in this article is that keeping fit has always been an integral part of a healthy lifestyle. This is the reason why the fitness business is worth around 3.7 trillion annually overall.

The best part is that there's plenty of money to earn from an online company by choosing the less-traveled route within this niche.

## 10. Music

Many new musicians are born each year. By the age of six years old about 28% will have studied a musical instrument.

The rate for 14-year-olds is more than 40 percent. That's does not include the rising number of individuals who begin playing instruments later in their lives. What we want to see here is that more people want or play use musical instruments.

All you need to do is present them with deals that they'll happily accept to pay for. That's the problem in the music industry In reality, lucrative programs are difficult to find. This is what we tried and some programs will offer up to 35 for each sale.

I also enjoy this particular niche since it's one of the niches in affiliate marketing that's always in flux and can be created into small websites that make income for many years and earn you the true passive income you're seeking in online marketing . There are many options for niche websites with a small budget to think of this broad field.

## 11. Weight Loss

helping people lose weight could be among the best methods to earn money online. In particular when you consider the fact that a significant percentage of both adults and children are currently classified as being overweight or obese pathologically.

In the end, everyone knows in their hearts that being overweight isn't a good thing for health. This is why a lot of people are searching for ways to lose those pounds by following a simple diet. But keep in mind, the majority of those in these categories are currently not convinced by diets or drinks which promise miraculous weight loss figures.

Instead, they are looking for an exercise program to lose weight to keep it off. That means you could use the information in this area with research from the fitness sector previously mentioned. In any case, the consumers who belong to this group spend an average of an average of $ 60 billion a year to shed weight.


12. Real estate There's a small amount of land that is habitable on this planet. The finite commodity has an increased market value, i.e. real estate is not reduced to zero. Yes, depressions and recessions could occur, and they can devalue the property.
However, nearly without exception the house price is getting back to levels prior to the recession. In the vicinity of 5 million homes are sold each year in an industry worth close to $ 30 trillion. There always exists a demand. The opportunity to earn money from sub-niches similar to the FSBO trend of a decade ago or in the luxury segment or various niches. In the end, there's no reason to be competitive with Zillow or Trulia within their own categories. You can instead concentrate on the countless informational questions (like What is it the best way to get a mortgage,

etc.) that have surprisingly low KD in these highly extremely competitive markets.

13. Debt settlement

A lot of people are in debts they are unable to pay or eliminate. As an example, there's at present $ 829 billion of consumer credit in the United States.

The majority of people dislike the idea of having to pay debts and are always looking for solutions. Wherever you come across problems or solutions I am sure that you will have the chance to earn money online from different sub-niche markets for debt settlement.

In this scenario it's through consolidating debt, credit score and offers from social finance. In this area there are affiliate programs that pay out $50, $100 and $ 150 for each lead.

14. Sports

Ah, the sports enthusiasts individuals who will pay excessive amounts of money to indulge in their pastime. Sometimes, it's just as an observer and not an athlete. It's fine in particular from a participant's point of perspective.

We know that it can be challenging to earn profits selling shoelaces and jockstraps. This is why we've created some awesome affiliate programs in sports for you which include the usual items like clothes and exercise equipment for different specialties in sports. Additionally, we have some interesting sports memorabilia, drinks services and affiliate programs. All of this will yield healthy profit for your company by being an affiliate marketing company.

15. Yoga

It wasn't too long ago that those looking to study yoga needed take their bags with them and go to an Ashram in India. Nowadays, the demand for yoga is so large that you will find numerous yoga centers in every major city and metropolis.

Yoga is becoming more sought-after than ever before as more people are seeking ways to unwind and attain some peace and tranquility by doing exercises to enhance their diet. Your task is to help them find products and services that can improve their yoga experience.

## 16. Airlines

We're big advocates of taking a look at the potential of a particular niche prior to investing your time and effort in creating an authoritative website around it. We did some research on about aviation in general, this caught our curiosity. We were awestruck. !!!!!

Did you have the knowledge that , in the US alone, 2.1 millions per minute are paid for travel by air?

The cost of air travel has become less expensive, and people are doing it more often for personal or commercial motives. It is important to note that profits margins in this business are incredibly thin. That means there is a large amount of affiliate commissions that must be paid out, but they are around $225 per sale.

## 17. Coffee

Did you have the knowledge that an average individual consumes at least three cups of coffee a throughout the day?

This could cost them $ 9 each day or $180 per

month. That's what they will spend on their coffee from 9-5. You could say that the coffee they drink is luxury today.

If you consider the possibility that they own a coffee grinder or percolator that they use at home or buy specialty coffee blends that you can be able to understand how the US coffee industry is estimated at around $ 75 billion per year.

Coffee is a small one of the foods we consume daily People can be extremely enthusiastic about it. It can be crazy, depending on how long it's been since they've run out of caffeine.

18. Make-up

One of the best ways to make money online is to find an area that is golden during good and bad times. A field where people can invest money even when they're broken.

Cosmetics and beauty are the perfect example of this specialty - sales are rising even in times of economic decline. Why? Since the average person is looking to be happy with how they look even if they cannot have the money for any other thing. The majority of people will invest money in this, even if they're in financial trouble.

It is now possible to say that local consumers buy makeup and there's no need to promote it on the internet.

19. Photography

It is possible that you don't have enough knowledge about photography to create an affiliate website related to the matter. Many photographers are hobbyists or amateurs. You don't need to be a professional photographer to be a successful blogger in this particular field. Another reason is that many bloggers have created their entire affiliate marketing company around their photography blogs. Do you doubt us? Google the name of a man who is named Joshua Dunlop.

Another benefit of working in this area is that photographers don't have to be hesitant about spending hundreds of dollars into the latest camera.

20. Supplements

Perhaps you've seen a slight trend in the niches that we've mentioned in the past?

Take note that some are connected in one way or another with health, food or luxurious. The insert sheet is a good illustration of this. The typical image of the term "supplement user" is that one drinks shakes of protein. However, this particular niche is different from this especially with regard to nootropics or what we refer to as "smart substances." In the simplest terms, this business is estimated to be approximately 120 billion dollars per year and will increase by a factor of 10 in the next 10 years. Don't overlook the fact that there are pet food supplements that are growing the market.

21. Insurance

Insurance is a strange field if you consider it. You're selling an individual financial security against anything that could occur. If the worst does not occur, the insurance company will cash out the profit.

This is the reason it is that the North American insurance industry is worth approximately 1.2 trillion annually. However, people are content to pay for the insurance because the average cost for the smallest car accident is about $7500.

The best part about the insurance industry is that it can be broken it into smaller categories like homeowners, auto health life, travel, pets etc. Volcan insurance is also available. It is true!

All you need to think about is thinking a little off-center to present an insurance affiliate program to an existing clientele.

22. Jewelry

This is an obvious niche. People are awestruck by jewelry. Jewelry costs money therefore there is an opportunity to earn money.

In reality, people from every walk of life buy on average $300 billion annually on rings, watches and bracelets. That's the principal reason that should be stressed that jewelry isn't only meant for "rich" or wealthy. Bling makes people feel good.

Nowadays, most jewelry is purchased to give as gifts to someone else, however around 30% of the jewelry sold globally is sold online by affiliates. Although there are stores selling jewelry in nearly every city, many people prefer shopping on the internet. Imagine that.

This is great news for you, particularly considering the fact that there are deals that offer a commission of $900 for each sale. This isn't a typo.

23. Auto

Certain niches might not inspire you to move your heart faster, but If you're an auto enthusiast then this is the ideal niche to pursue - it is a way to combine something that you value and the possibility of earning an all-time salary through related programs.

The options are diverse that range from motorcycles to motorbikes and golf cars.

24. Baby products

If you're unsure whether the baby niche suitable for you, here's few things to bear in mind: As you read this article, 20 babies have been born.

Are you skeptical? Check out the global population count and you'll be able to see it is growing.

It's not just the fact that most newborn parents spend around 10,000 dollars in the first year of their life, looking after their newborn baby.

What are the most popular niches you can think of that people would have an obligation morally to invest money in? I'm with you.

25. Bitcoin and other cryptos

I'm incredibly pleased with how cryptocurrency have helped to alter the FIAT market for currencies. Because they were perturbed.

Even though you've witnessed Bitcoin fluctuate and then plummet completely, cryptocurrency is in the game to stay.

Bitcoin as an example has experienced a remarkable growth in the past six months. This implies it means that "enthusiasm" is not ending. Therefore, you're still an early adopter when you are able to reach this market early enough.

## Chapter 4 How To Market And Earn Sales For No Cost

The most crucial aspect of having an account an active user on Instagram will be growing your followers to ensure that you have an a marketable audience! While every other aspect that is in this guide has some way or another helped the ability of you to increase your following and improve your reach however, there are a number of actions you can take to increase the number of followers on your Instagram account, and begin to see more engagement. In this section, you will learn how to increase your followers and begin generating revenue via the use of your Instagram account. Encourage Engagement On Your Account The initial step you can take to build your following is to get people to take part via your profile. Keep in mind that Instagram's Instagram algorithm favors people who interact with other pages. This means that when you encourage your followers to begin engaging more with you, it is likely that they'll see more of your posts too. Engaging your followers can be done in two ways: by engaging with other users and inviting the participation of your followers.

When you are interacting with followers regularly they are more likely to interact with your blog posts since they can feel the building of a relationship. The constant exchange of messages between your readers becomes a regular element of your interaction. If you make the effort to browse through your followers list and engage with them, you "break the cold" between you and them and make them feel more at ease and more engaged with your brand. This can be done by regularly looking through your followers' list and clicking on various accounts and engaging with their posts. Commenting with a heartfelt message and liking their latest posts can be a great way to engage with your followers and encourage them to connect with you next time they encounter your posts. While you are posting you could also ask for feedback by saying things such as "We are loving summer! Do you?" that encourages users to say, "Yes" or answer an answer on your profile photo. You can also encourage engagement by creating captions that read: "Comment your favorite _____!" or "Tag someone you know who would enjoy this!"

Engaging your audience with your content this way will help them stop their mental process of scrolling through their feeds and instead choose to interact with what you have to say instead. Another way to increase participation is to host giveaways on your website and establish rules that require people to take part in your post in order to be entered into the prize. In most cases, businesses choose the prize that they wish to offer and then set the conditions for people to participate in the giveaway as, "Follow us, tag an acquaintance, and post this post on your social media accounts in order to enter into the contest!" They will then keep the giveaway open for a specific duration of time, allowing them to see a great deal of interaction from their followers. This type of strategy boosts engagement on particular post, but it will help you drive up the engagement on your other posts too. It is not a good idea to participate in too many giveaways however, 2 to 4 giveaways per year is plenty and the best way to get engaged with your followers.

Always updating your Following List The people and hashtags that you follow will appear on your main screen. This allows you to view images that everyone you're following posts frequently. It is essential to ensure that you're frequently updating your list of followers to ensure that you're only getting people who are in fact associated with your brand's identity or your positioning. You may be inspired to follow your personal interests on Instagram However, it's best for personal accounts that are private instead of corporate accounts. It is important to ensure that time looking through your followers' accounts is used to invest into the growth of your business , so that what the time you spend scrolling becomes more efficient in the end. You can make changes to your following lists by going through it and then unfollowing any account that does not fit with your branding. In this way, you're not consuming content that is entirely irrelevant to your brand or following accounts that will not provide you with any benefits from your efforts. You are able to follow and unfollow up to 60 accounts within an hour, so make sure you take your time and keep doing it on a regular basis to ensure that you don't have many chances of making the connection to your account. It is recommended to do this every week to ensure you're staying relevant to your field and keeping track of the most recent trends and individuals who are emerging. After you have removed all accounts that aren't important to you, begin to look through the most popular hashtags on your list and check if there are brand new followers or hashtags that you can you to keep an eye on by looking at the most popular posts in these search results. This way, you'll begin to follow new users who might help in bringing greater attention to your account every time you read their posts and interact.

In addition, if you keep track of the latest hashtags that are popular in your field it is also possible to begin applying those hashtags to your photos to stay relevant too. This kind of research can create two opportunities to grow all in one go This is why it's worthy of your attention and time! If you want to be able to say the right things at the appropriate time on Instagram It is essential be sure that you're posting the right thing at the right time. By posting relevant content at the right time, you will ensure that you are pertinent and ensure that your content is relevant to what your followers are contemplating or going through so that they will be interested and engaged with your posts. The easiest method to do the appropriate thing at the right moment on Instagram is to follow your followers and keeping an eye on the most recent trends, issues and concerns that might be emerging that people are watching. For instance, if, for example, you're involved in blogging and you write about current events related to famous personalities it is important to keep up-to-date with all of the latest developments and gossip and writing about them when they appear in your attention. Similar is true in any industry you're in. If you spot an emerging trend or topic that is sweeping across your field it is important to be prepared to join involved and tailor the way you communicate it in line with your own branding, and implementing the information as quickly as you can. Alongside keeping track of the unexpected developments that occur in your field You should also keep track of trends that are expected, such as holidays or scheduled events relevant to your customers. If, for instance, you work working in the fashion sector you must be paying attention to fashion-related events such as Fashion Week and the Victoria Secret Fashion Show. If you're working in the tech sector You should pay close attention to the latest gadget launches as well as information about important events in the tech sector including the annual E3 event.

These kinds of events happen frequently and

are useful in helping you remain relevant to your market by being aware of the information shared by those who are driving the industry such as influencers or developers. It is essential to not discuss things out of the norm or in your own lane, as the sharing of information that is that is too long after the event has took place could lead to you being perceived as unimportant or out of date. People who are exposed to organizations sharing outdated information think that the company is not paying enough attention or isn't genuinely interested enough to remain up-to-date with the latest developments in their particular field. This is why people don't follow you. We are living in a digital world where information is readily available and trends can change and then fall faster. You must be prepared to embrace these trends and begin creating your brand's image in the instant of the moment, but not just after the information or trend has already begun to decline in the market. If you are finding that keeping up-to-date is more difficult than it seems you might want to find three to four blogs or people to follow that are eager to be on the cutting edge of the latest trends. Only pay attention to these people or other resources.

In this way, you're not putting yourself in a position of overwhelm by following more than one person at a time and getting overwhelmed by what's relevant and what's an emerging trend, and what's totally irrelevant to you and your followers. Aiming at Your Audience with Your words You've probably figured out that the most effective way for Instagram to reach out to audiences is via hashtags. This is the way to reach new users and begin increasing your followers quickly. But there's a second aspect of language that is important in creating an impact with your captions and writing and that is through using words that resonate with your followers. It is not a good idea to use words that don't resonate with your target audience or are completely uninteresting or outdated, since it will result in your viewers becoming bored the content you write and struggling to "follow" the message you're trying to communicate to them. The best way to communicate as your audience would be to be attentive to what they're interested in by being a follower and listening to what they're saying. Always browse through your feed and take the time to read what people you follow are talking about to learn more about the way they speak and the way they frame their message and if they use specific slang words or phrases that they employ to engage their audience. When you spend time reading the captions of your target audience's comments and captions, the more you're getting to know the way they speak and what they are talking about, and what they're reading. That way, you'll be able to start resembling their language with your own posts and expressing things in a manner that is understandable to your readers.

If you do decide to emulate your audience There are some things you be able to avoid doing so that your audience lose interest in what you're saying. The main thing to remember is to be careful not to imitate your audience until you lose your authenticity due to the fact that it sounds like you're exactly like the ones are reading. You must take note of the voice of your company and its mission statement , and then adapt the language of your industry to match your own tone, not vice versa. If your tone seems out of line with your industry it is possible to consider changing it to suit the needs of your industry, however, don't alter your style too often or you'll come off as untrustworthy and fake. Another thing you must avoid is creating content which are stuffed with terms that your followers aren't likely to grasp.

If you try to make use of industry terminology that is widely used by the people selling services and products within the industry but isn't likely to be recognized by those who buy from or follow the business, you could lose followers simply because they aren't able to know what you are talking about. You don't want to cause gaps and confusion by using a language your target audience doesn't understand as it can make it difficult for your customers to follow you and to support your business. Make it clear, communicate in a manner that your audience understands and also adapt the language to fit the message and goal of your brand. Making use of Instagram Stories Instagram Stories are an effective device that can be used to build your existing audience but also to attract new customers to your company. If you utilize your Instagram stories in the right way you will be able to create massive amounts of followers' engagement as well as provide them with an opportunity to engage to your brand and build an engaging page overall. In Instagram users are prone to engaging with brands they like and consume the most the content they are able to. Instagram provides a variety of opportunities for users to do this. When you post videos throughout the day it creates your followers with the chance to feel as if you truly care of them all day, creating the feeling of caring and love among your fans and you. This will not only keep your current followers, but it'll aid in helping new followers realize how engaging and close you are to your audience, which will lead to them wanting to become a part of your community also! The reason stories work is that people are curious, and they want to know the insider's secrets. This isn't a negative thing , it's simply a human trait that we all want to be part of something larger than us, and we desire to be connected with others that surround us to be part of the "something larger." You can present your self as the facilitator of the "something larger" by transforming your brand into a memorable experience users will enjoy and an entity they are able to share an intimate and meaningful connection with. Stories offer a wonderful way to accomplish this since every photo or video you post reflects a piece of your own behind-the-scenes experience. You can also arrange your feed to provide a more personal and intimate experience by sharing items that make others feel as if they're connected to you via your feed.

The secret to making your stories personal and using your followers to gain new ones and keep those you already have is to ensure that the content you post in your stories is unique and distinct from what you're sharing elsewhere. Be sure to share items that are more intimate and "private" as opposed to what you post on IGTV or your own feed because the users feel as if they are truly getting that private view into your business. Stories on Instagram are already exclusive since they are only available for 24 hours. they're gone and can't be seen again. You can increase this exclusivity by sharing relevant content, by mentioning items that you've shared in your stories earlier, which your new followers will not see anymore, or even by declaring that your feed is exclusive. Use phrases like "Keep your eyes open for my stories, because I'm gonna announce an exclusive offer right here... You can get it three days before simply through watching my story!" Or something like that. Another way you can truly benefit from Instagram stories is to make stories that highlight your story, allowing new followers to view exclusive details from your earlier stories.

So, if you're an individual who frequently travels and is often sharing intimate travel experiences with others including the restaurants you eat at or people whom you meet, then you should think about sharing these experiences in your stories. You can then create the highlights of some of the moments of your travels that were particularly engaging or exciting to ensure that your audience can look back over your stories and begin to feel more connected to your brand right away. Making use of your highlight reels in this manner is an excellent opportunity to let your new viewers what to expect and giving them the feeling of knowing your brand and you for a long time and build their trust in you from the beginning. Utilizing IGTV to Grow Your Followership IGTV is an excellent method to grow your followership, as the videos are in place until you remove them so that people can go back to your IGTV channel to watch content that you posted for weeks, days, months perhaps even years earlier if it's been up for enough. It is possible to use IGTV to attract new followers by making great IGTV videos, and then promoting them across the web so that users tend to go to your channel and view. When they view your video and are impressed by the quality of your content you create, they may decide to follow your blog to gain more followers If they decide to enjoy your channel. The biggest benefit of IGTV is the fact that you are able to advertise your IGTV channel in the same way as you would with a YouTube channel, or any other video content for free on the internet.

# Chapter 5: Top Best Affiliate Programs 1. Best Affiliate Programs For Bloggers

1. Amazon Associates
   The internet is huge in the world of eCommerce its worldwide popularity continues to grow.

   Thus, if you ever talk about products that could be offered for sale on Amazon.com then it is logical for you to sign up for Amazon.com.

   Associates to begin earning smaller commissions on products or services customers purchase when they click on the Amazon affiliate links. it works by sharing products and programs that are readily available on Amazon.com to your targeted market through targeted links and then you earn up to 10% up front each time a customer buys.

2. Shopify

Shopify is the most known e-commerce website builder, with 500 000 sellers and more than 150% of commissions on paid suppliers.

However, you should be knowledgeable about the business before recommending it to your market.

The payment method is PayPal.
3. BigCommerce
BigCommerce is a different eCommerce system that provides of the tools required to build, manage, and grow an online store.

It is among the top eCommerce platforms available together with Shopify and offers a variety of built-in functions as well as information tools that can assist small-scale business owners in creating an effective online shop and increase the rate at which they convert.

Commission Price: Up 200 percent of client's initial month-to-month payment or as high as $1,500 for each venture user you recommend

Payment Options: Straight down payment or wire transfer

Modal Payment: $1.50 per lead, flat fee. Also, $40 for each business lead

User Support Yes

Market Reputation: Excellent

The nature of Commission Referrals will only be considered when they are made within 90 days from the time you use your associate link. Once approved, transactions are paid at when they are secured.

4. ClickBank:

The company has been running for

more than a quarter of a century. It is home to thousands of customers spread over 190 countries.

The network is quite simple to join. It is open to anyone who has blogs or websites on the network. Additionally currently, there are a variety of associate-related products and services that you can choose from. The commissions are definitely very high, approximately 75% of every purchase made through the associate hyperlink.

But, the system has drawbacks. There are a few issues with slow-moving consumer feedbacks and regular charges for accounts that are not active.

2.BEST Affiliate Programs for Beginners
1. Ebay
The eBay Associate Network is eBay's affiliate advertising program.

If you sign up and begin sharing your listings with other sellers beyond eBay it is possible to increase your profits by diversifying your revenue streams and even get an credit score for your fee of final value when you sell your item , and also when the item actually sells.

Niche: Online Market

Commission Prices: 45 to 75 percent of ebay.com profit share. Reactivated or new ebay.com customers can increase their commission cost.

Payment Method: PayPal or direct deposit
Type of Payment The payment is made month-to-month if a minimum of $10 is met.
Customer Assistance Customer Assistance: Yes
Market Reputation: Outstanding
2. Fiverr

Fiverr is known as the world's largest targeted market for digital services that are available online.

Fiverr is by far the biggest marketplace for self-employed online solutions. From design to marketing to technology, there's a solution available for all needs

It's incredibly easy to earn money on Fiver. You just earn money by driving traffic to your site.
Earn money from online advertising services by the creation of logos, logos the logo, etc.

It's completely free to start Start here.
Fiverr Affiliate Benefits
* Maximum Earnings
* Professional Support
* Intuitive Dashboards
* Creative Resources

## 3. ONLINE COURSES FOR AFFILIATE PROGRAM

### 1. Coursera

Increase to 20-25% of commission through Coursera.

Coursera is a software which offers 1000 training classes and even focuses on courses that focus on digital advertising, web content marketing and content advertising and personal growth.

The associate program is based with it's Url share network, as and offers you up to 20% to 25% discount.

Moreso, as a Coursera affiliate, you secure free access in order to professionally-designed banners and even a monthly associate newsletter with curated material referrals.

The Goals of Coursera:

* Get the most up-to-date skills
* Prepare yourself to be a professional

* Earn a certificate or degree
* Educate your team

2. Teachable
Teachable can help you create and sell your online-based programs.

Teachable's partner courses pay monthly payments up to 30 percent.
3. Udemy

What is the actual associate program?

It is the Udemy associate programme is an internal marketing plan that searches for people who are able to easily promote udemy programs to earn payment. Of the many applicants they filter and select the ones who can market their the courses to their customers.

The associates selected are granted access to exclusive content to help them find the most lucrative deals they can advertise. In simple terms the benefits of being an Udemy Associate, especially when your already own an existing web website or are complying with the rules the guidelines, is that you generally receive a 20 percent commission on every program bought by students of Udemy student using your Udemy affiliate link within seven days of clicking the link.

Udemy offers you advertising materials such as Udemy banners and voucher codes that you can use to market your training courses. Udemy Associate Marketing definitely a warm and helpful program.

4. Web hosting affiliate program
Every great website calls for hosting. Most bloggers or even marketers who write about what they do , sign to webhosting companies at first. However, you need to be aware and

agree with the company before you can recommend the service to your market.

Top webhosting affiliate affiliate programs as that are listed below:
1. Bluehost Affiliate Program
This is a very admired webhosting provider, and has been proven to be the most effective method to earn affiliate programs money.
Website hosting platforms are also among the top affiliate programs that pay in existence, with payouts of between $65 and $120 for each sale. Also, one of the most successful webhosting affiliate programs are the Bluehost associate program.

Bluehost offers three kinds of plans for hosting:

1. Hosting shared by a third party:
A fundamental hosting preparation for specific blogs or sites.

2. VPS Hosting:
Digital Exclusive Web Servers to host larger internet sites, with robust features.

3. Committed Website hosting:
High power and high time to uptime by using custom-designed servers.

2. Hostgator Affiliate Program

HostGator Affiliate Program HostGator associate program stands among the most popular and popular associate programs.

It also has the structure of a commission based on performance which the company pays a large amount of conversions; the general commission begins at $49.

Selling prepares for VPS hosting websites, WordPress website hosting, cloud hosting for websites in addition

to dedicated account hosting.
HostGator utilizes Impact Radius to run
its affiliate program.
Around $120 in payouts.

5. Website builder affiliate program
1. Wix
Many people use Wix to build their
websites It's the top website or blog
construction company, with many
hundred million users.

Furthermore, using Wix is one of the
simplest (as as well as cost-effective)
methods to build an uncomplicated
website that can include and earn
money from affiliate web hyperlinks.

Commission And Settlement Details:
As an official Wix associate, you'll
definitely earn upto $100 per
customer. The Wix will definitely pay

on a monthly basis. You must have the minimum of $300 in order for withdrawal of funds.

2. Weebly

Weebly is a fully-featured platform that allows users to establish and grow their small online company, with carefully curated website designs, eCommerce capabilities, as well as integrated marketing.

About 40 % of business proprietors are using Weebly with over 325 million unique users each month. Options range from free to $25 per month, with business-oriented options too.

Commission: 30%.
Cookie: Up to 120 days.
3. Attractive

Strikingly is highly regarded by many business leaders and creatives.

Their popular receptive styles instantly adjust to look amazing on any device.
* You can launch your website in less than 30 minutes with no programming or layout skills needed. The attributes include domain simple stores with no costs for purchase, blogs analytics, register/call types, social feeds and more.
They also offer a wide range of marketing products and support to assist you convert more leads.

## Chapter 6: Promotion Of Your Brand And Building Trust

From SEO and Content Marketing, through Building a List Building as well as Social Media If you're not a millionaire There's a limit to what you can accomplish using PPC advertising by itself. In the end, affiliate marketing is about being in a position to promote your site and your business and connect with a wider population. This involves leveraging your email list, your blog, and social media accounts you've created as well as using these to draw new customers and increase trust and authority.

What you must be aware of here is that you're the middle man - and in all businesses the role of'middleman is in fact useless. The customer isn't really in need of you, and neither does the seller necessarily need you, which is why you must become indispensable to every. In this instance, it means helping the person who created the product to market a larger quantity of their products than they normally would. For the customer this means providing high quality information and content, and assisting in finding the most beneficial bargains and products. Each business is based on offering value in one form of the other. This is why the online marketer adds worth. In addition it's what makes you a successful online marketer and create momentum and build a following.

This chapter you will be able to see this connection clearly as we look at the three major types of marketing options available for you to help advertise your business.

How to Make it Work on Social Media

One of the most effective tools for affiliate marketers are social networks. This provides you with the ability to communicate directly but at the same making use of the power of social networks in the real world.

In comparison to e-mail marketing, the social network comes with the disadvantage of having to must use an outside party, that is Facebook, Twitter or Google. While this could be problematic but the good thing is that users can share your content with acquaintances, which makes it more likely to become viral. However social media tends to be multi-media, which allows you to share different kinds of content.

However, the majority of companies and marketers do their social media marketing in a completely wrong manner. The problem is that they'll spend the time on social media, but what they will talk about is how successful their business is . It is very similar to corporate language..

The type of information you're likely to receive, are remarks like: "Find out why our EPOS system is the most effective in the market!"

"Save your time and money by using a more efficient EPOS technology!"

"Looking to purchase the perfect EPOS system? Do you want to choose the best software program available on the market!"

If you are posting this kind of status that you're posting on or on your Twitter or Facebook account, then you're completely not achieving the primary goal of social marketing via media.

This type of content could be fine when you already have an audience and the goal was to only advertise to them. (Even in that case there's a chance that you'd lose some of your subscribers who will quickly unsubscribe. ...) What's happening, however is that you're publishing content to no one and not offering anyone who could find it any reason to think that they should sign up. The first question you must be asking yourself when you're creating content for the internet is: Would you be a follower of the account? If you came across an account on social media like this, would you be a subscriber?

If you don't then you have to think about what you are doing to increase your worth.

How to Use Social Media Right

The most important thing is the way you view your social media profiles and the way you think about it in the larger perspective in your overall marketing. Particularly, it's crucial to begin thinking of your social media accounts not as just a means to advertise yourself, but as an actual product on its own. What does this mean? It is a sign that the social media accounts must offer an advantage to the point that people are enticed to join them and be disappointed when they went away. Naturally, you must keep focused on your marketing goals which means that you have concentrate on the field or niche you've decided to go with. If it's fitness, it's not a good idea for you to make your Facebook page to become exclusively about business. However, it's not ideal to make your profile focused on how excellent the product you're selling. Instead, you should try to create an account that is filled with inspirational pictures of people exercising and getting in shape along with interesting information about truly fascinating new products, and with useful tips and suggestions.

In the event that you're selling insurance for life you'll probably find it's difficult to think of ways to keep an engaging and informative social media profile. If that's the case it's not difficult to think outside the box. This could involve sharing photos of families enjoying their time together, or suggestions to make your family more active. Perhaps you manage a social media page that offers 'tips for modern parent' or you might offer a humorous perspective "dispatches from the frontline in parenting'. Whatever you choose, you've created a brand that's almost new and mission statement and a fresh kind of value for the social media account and you've convinced people to follow your account. This is how you develop your following. You will find that if you consistently publish high-quality content in this way and it will eventually give you an enormous number of people to market to. What's important is the value you're offering.

Other Ways to Deliver Value

There are many ways to provide the value. One way is to simply share many great pieces of content. This includes sharing your personal content (more on the subject later) but it could be sharing articles from other blogs within your area of expertise. This implies that you're offering a curated content service that keeps your readers updated with the most recent news as well as breakthroughs and products within your area.

The best thing about sharing content you did not create is that it offers many benefits while simultaneously taking just a few minutes. If you are a frequent user of YouTube and Reddit early in the morning You can click "share" to publish on your Facebook or Twitter feed, and thus give your followers excellent content.

Another advantage that comes with sharing content from third-party sources is the ability to make certain that what you're selling likely to be successful. Similar to choosing the best affiliate products for your business It is virtually impossible to guarantee that the content won't be successful since you can see that it's being read, liked and shared.

One of the most effective methods to accomplish this is via Reddit because this website is a social network which lets you know how content is "upvoted" (similar to an similar site). Another option is to utilize an automated tool such as BuzzSumo, which will show the reader how each blog post is performing in various forms of social media, and allows you to easily share on your own blogs.

How SEO Functions
So , how can SEO function?
In the most basic sense, SEO works via 'robots and spiders'. These are the programs and scripts that Google utilizes to "read" the web. These programs work as a team and let Google to index websites by adding URLs of websites as well as their content to a database it could utilize to show relevant results when someone conducts the search. While reading web page's content, Google will comb through it for words and phrases and then these will be matched to the search terms. If someone is searching for 'I'm looking for an additional hat with my blue pants If you have the exact phrase on your website (or an equivalent phrase) it is then displayed in the most relevant results. It's referred to as a "long tail keyword'. It's considered a keyword because it's a keyword that was searched by someone who wanted to locate your website and it's a long tail due to it being lengthy-form - a type of keyword that is naturally found in

the content, and that very isn't likely to be competing with you on.

The most effective way to receive many hits from these long-tail keywords is to write plenty of articles on your topic. This is the reason why the majority of websites have blogs The more content you put on blogs, the more content is available to Google to crawl which means the better chance it will show up on various search results.

Keywords that are regular - or those which you'll be targeting specifically will be shorter. A good example of this could be 'buy hats on the internet'. This is the kind of things that many people look up frequently, but for which there is also plenty of competition. The question is how can you position yourself for these terms so that you'll be higher than your competition using the same keywords? The answer is repetition and volume: simply having lots of content can help to beat the competition with lesseffort, as will repetition of your keywords more often. It is not advisable to repeatedly repeat the keywords however, as it appears to Google as if you're trying to manipulate results and artificially increase your rank in the absence of quality content (content isn't always be read with ease when there are hundreds of times the same phrase. This is known as keyword stuffing. '!). It is generally suggested that your keyword has approximately 1-2% keyword density'. This means that you could use your keyword more than once every 100 to 200 words. If you're looking to play it safe to avoid being penalized, you might want to be more careful than this.

To use the same keywords repeatedly without worry of being'stuffed', an easy solution is to create more information. With 100 posts on your subject it is possible to utilize a very low amount of density, and still use the keywords many times on your website.

Additionally, keywords can be utilized to enhance also the HTML of your website and in the file names. Make use of keywords in your images' names as well as for your page names , and this will strengthen your relationship with Google. It is also important to note that Google considers certain content to be more important to the subject of a site than other depending on its location. This implies that content found that is in the closing or opening paragraphs of your blog post is considered to be more relevant than content found in the body. Utilizing the keywords within your H1 or H2 tag will have the same effect, since they are both titles.

Link Building

The robots and spiders discover information by looking for hyperlinks on other websites. If there aren't any links that point to your site from a pages that Google has already found, then it has no idea that your content exists and it could not show on the search results in the end.

However the hyperlinks (called "inbound" links) have another purpose in that they serve as testimonials or references. If the website linking to your site the website must consider your content to be relevant or intriguing. If many high-profile websites link to your site this could mean they're on the right track. This is the basic idea however, as with the density of keywords, it is essential to never modify this process. Sites that have a massive amount of poor quality links are penalized, for example and so will websites who attempt to buy links, websites that just ever exchange links, and 'blog networks' which connect to one another in the form of a chain.

Optimization

In addition, a great SEO strategy should also incorporate an optimization of the website as a whole. It means that the site must load quickly, be responsive to ensure that it appears good on any display (including mobile phones) and must be easy to navigate, and not suffocating in ads.

This is essential as Google is determined to make sure that the websites that it provides visitors with offer a great experience, regardless of what kind of device they're using. Additionally, if your website is designed an orderly manner, this could in making it easy for Google's spiders navigate. The presence of a "site map" for instance , can be extremely beneficial since it makes sure that Google does not miss any information within your site's overall.

The Process

With that in mind the basic process for SEO is to include tons of quality blog posts to your website frequently, with keywords, and making sure you get as many hyperlinks as you can on other websites that relate to your site.

As an affiliate marketer it's not the best idea to invest all of your time working on this, since there are better methods to increase direct traffic. However, you can make an excellent ROI just adding content (which also has other applications as we'll discover) and trying to gain hyperlinks on some of the more popular blogs that are in your field. This can be accomplished through guest posts. This is where you offer an article on your topic with content that is free, with the condition that they give the link to your site in exchange. In this way, they receive free content, and you receive free links. Start with blogs similar to yours. As you progress and gain experience, you can begin targeting larger and better websites. A single link on the correct website could completely alter your luck and you should not underestimate the power of this method.

However creating a website efficiently using WordPress can ensure you get the best speed of loading, fast loading times, and a flexible design.

More PPC

Google AdWords

We've previously discussed the best way to utilize Facebook Ads to promote PPC, but this is just one form of PPC. Another site that offers an identical service is Google, which is a hugely popular AdWords'. AdWords is a combination of Google AdWords on Facebook and SEO basically letting you pay per click advertisements that are displayed on specific SERPs (Search Engine Results Pages). You select the keywords you wish to target, then pay for an advertisement and see your results appear just above the organic results , as"sponsored results".

Quick Lektion: AdWords as Research Instrument

It's interesting to note that you can utilize AdWords as a tool for research prior to executing your SEO. Be aware that it could take quite a while to master SEO and also to reach the top of organic results for search It's important to be sure your keywords are worth ranking before you put into all that time and effort , or before you hire someone for an enormous amount of money to perform it for you.

Therefore, you must take into consideration taking advantage of AdWords as an outcome tool, by testing the search terms you'd like to rank on to be AdWords keywords. If the ads generate large amounts of money that's worth looking into the organic results. If not? Try different keywords to see if they are more successful. If you discover a keyword that's profitable, you'll know that it's worthwhile to put in the effort.

Utilizing AdWords rather than Facebook Ads has distinct advantages. It means, for instance, that you can make your ads more relevant to visitors who are searching for the kind of content that you offer. In addition you'll also be able to use specific tools you can utilize to improve your marketing campaign. For example, Google 'Remarketing' targets users who have already come to your site and have visited the same page. One illustration of how this can be utilized is to retarget those who have spent time browsing your book with ads for the exact same eBook. This is a tremendously efficient way to promote since the person is already aware of the product you're selling and won't click through your advertisement except if they're interested in purchasing the item.

Another distinctive feature of AdWords is the fact that it allows you use "negative keywords". These are words that are important to remove to ensure that your ads do not be displayed. A good example of this would be to eliminate the word "free" in this way, you won't spend time advertising to people who have explicitly stated that they don't want to make a purchase.

AdWords also works to Google Analytics which provides you with tons of information and statistics that you can't receive from Facebook. One example of what you can accomplish with an Analytics account as well as your AdWords account is create goals, for instance, a customer purchasing your book. You can then check the control panels of your account to determine the ads that are producing the most conversions not just the ones that get the most clicks. This type of information allows you to refine your advertising campaign to a greater extent and significantly increase the effectiveness of your campaign as time passes.

CPA

But, Facebook does have a feature that's somewhat similar to goals and it could be considered more effective.

In particular, Facebook gives you some basic CPA functions. CPA is a shorthand for "Cost Per Action' and what it signifies is you're not more paying per click however, you're instead paying per specific action. A single action could range that involves someone purchasing the product (or in the case of Facebook redemption of a deal) or signing up to the mailing list. This is what makes Facebook something like an affiliate!

It's not an easy task to establish affiliate sales

as your method of action. It's not possible to guarantee an ROI with a scenario that you only pay when someone purchases your affiliate item.

However, it is an extremely useful method to build your mainlining list. It also implies that you're paying X dollars per subscriber. You can also use this to boost your Facebook page's likes. These can translate into conversions at a minimum.

There are a variety of CPA websites which specialize in this type of service, and are more flexible due to this. These comprise MaxBounty, Ascend Media, AdWorkMedia and many more. While it's a great concept the market isn't as well-developed as PPC in general, which means there's no single platform that's yet to rise to the top of the pile. The majority of CPA networks can be difficult to navigate at first, and some are associated with shady practices.

For the more experienced marketers, this is definitely an area worth keeping in mind!

# Chapter 7: Off-Page Seo And Strategies For Backlinking

Creating backlinks is at the core of off-page SEO, and we'll discuss the process (building links) in great detail in the following chapter, off-page optimization encompasses more than just building backlinks.

Off-Page SEO 101

If you Google the phrase "off-page SEO" it is the very first term that appears in SERP is off-page SEO, which refers to off-page strategies that are used to increase search rank for specific pieces of content in Google SERP. From this we can see that, even while back linking (link creation) is a significant aspect SEO off-page is more important, even though the specific elements it covers are open to interpret.

It begs the question, what is off-page SEO exactly? One of the main aspects is that it covers the building of links. Beyond that, /r/bigSEO the subreddit of SEO declares the term "off-page" SEO is everything that is not part of any optimization performed on-page. It covers all things that are not directly related to optimizing your website's content and pages using keywords or multimedia, preparing your website to achieve the highest load speed, making use of HTML tags and the many other elements we have discussed previously in our chapter SEO on-page.

Off-page SEO, in essence, refers to how much exposure you can bring to your website and content. Imagine it as follows. The more exposure your content receives the more it will impact other elements of your website, such as links or citations, bounce rates as well as other elements such as back and mentions hyperlinks.

Consider an instance in which you have created the top topic-based resource available in your field. If you can do this you increase the chance of other experts in the field to cite your valuable resource rises and as a result your chances of being in the top SERPs increase.

Ahrefs one of the Internet's most prominent leaders in all things SEO describes Off-page

SEO to mean "every marketing strategy that is used on a site and which can alter the way Google search spiders place pages on its index."

As mentioned previously linking is a distinct part that is linked building. In addition, off-page SEO also includes the following aspects--we'll discuss these aspects and how they build that leads to link building:

Guest Blogging

Guest blogging is among the most effective methods to present your website's specialization to a potential audience that might otherwise have been unaware of your useful content and pages.

Unfortunately, because of certain marketers who make use of guest blogging, it's earned been criticized as a unethical method to gain publicity and back links to your website. If done properly it's not, and in fact, it is one of the most efficient methods to be noticed by the masses and drive traffic to your site of interest and create important back links.

When you use guest blogging, avoid making use of it solely for the reason of creating links since over time this has evolved into an unprofessional link building technique which Webmasters (and Google Spiders) frown on and can have your niche-specific affiliate site being penalized.

Engaging in guest blogging with the intention of contributing to a particular topic or community offers many benefits. In the beginning, it can help to build consciousness, i.e. when done properly it exposes your thoughts and your niche website to a crowd that is looking for solutions and answers. Additionally, it increases the visibility of your brand, and affects various aspects of SEO like naturally-generated backlinks, and brings an increase in referral traffic and is, in fact, good to build links.

Take a look at an example.

If you are a contributor to a popular blog or a niche website on such topics as, for example of weight loss using vegans You are exposing your self to the audience of that website and as a result you increase your authority. Furthermore, because people will want to learn what they can about the individual who made this amazing contribution, you'll be rewarded with referral traffic.

The Back Linking 101: What is and why it's important

We have previously discussed the importance of ensuring an excellent UX by ensuring that , once an audience/Google search robot lands on your page or content pieces, it is simple to navigate to the next element or part of your website. We referred to this as internal linking, and discovered how internal links are the ideal method of doing this.

Internal linking is a crucial aspect to ensure your site is crawlable and simple to navigate Back hyperlinks, i.e. links that direct users to your website's content and pages are among the most crucial kinds of links that you must to build if your target website is to be at the top in SERP for particular keywords.

Backlinking is so crucial that even now, Google still sees back links as a signal of relevance, importance and popularity. The quality of backlinks is more important than the number, but the higher quality of backlinks an internet site has the higher

Google thinks it is relevant to a specific phrase and the more favorable it evaluates the website in terms of its the ranking.

In the above picture it is clear that the term "backlink" refers to an external link that links to a part of content on your site of interest. Backlinks occur when, because of the belief that your pages or content will be useful to other webmasters point their viewers to your site's pages or content.

Backlinks are among the most important factors Google utilizes to determine the spot on their index they will give to websites. From the standpoint of search engines we can think of backlinks as "streets" search bots utilize to navigate around the internet and connect related topics and pages. If a piece or page of content contains many "streets" (or links) that point at it Google interprets it to be a sign that the content, or the page of content is pertinent and valuable, due to that, Google is likely to give the page or content a higher position.

In a variety of instances, you've heard the phrase Google spiders. This is a reference to the complex algorithms Google utilizes to search the internet. Search spiders make use of these backlinks in order to understand the ways in which pages are linked to each other and the queries that are made by their users. Search spiders use backlinks, i.e. the number of links that link back to a web page as well as the value of those links with respect to the websites they are getting them from, in order to determine the quality and credibility of a particular page or content. Nowadays, search algorithms have advanced to the point that they're now competent of determining the authority and credibility of an backlink. If you build a lot of quality backlinks that originate from trusted websites, Google takes this as an endorsement of your trustworthiness which increases the rank of your website and your organic traffic.

Beyond what we've talked about above We will look at the ways in which back linking can be very advantageous for the affiliate marketing professional.

The Backlink Strategy: What to Do? Develop Contextual Backlinks

The first thing to do is:

Whatever way your site's niche is ranked however tempting an offer may be, do not purchase backlinks. Also, do not purchase BACKLINKS. If you do, you'll have to pay for it. Due to the need to diversify their link portfolios In order to diversify their link portfolio, affiliate marketers typically find themselves purchasing the backlink services. Certain of these are legitimate as the hyperlinks they offer are of high-quality and are from trusted sites. However, the majority of them aren't genuine and offer thousands of spam links and their use can result in penalties and even de-indexing.

Before you purchase hyperlinks from the "marketer" promising to aid you in ranking first in search results for keywords with 700k average monthly search volume be aware that search algorithms have developed in such a way that they are able to discern the difference between an authentic backlink and one specifically designed with the purpose of manipulating the system.

Imagine it in this manner.

If Google Spiders notice that your link profile has grown exponentially in just a few days it is likely that they find out that you're employing unethical methods to build links that Google does not like and encourages webmasters to do because Google prefers natural hyperlinks. The most important thing to remember is that an organic link profile is similar to a plant that is growing and grows over time. Because 100 people cannot read your website's content simultaneously and also decide that they want to hyperlink back to your site simultaneously Any website that employs link-building techniques that do not comply with Google guidelines is likely to be slapped with the wrath Google by de-indexing.

What can you do to make a solid link profile that will allow you to climb to the top on the SERP for the keywords you want to rank for? This is accomplished by applying the strategies listed below:

Content Marketing

Even after the many Google Content Updates is still an important element in the way Google decides where to index content and pages is the reason why content marketing is an essential part of linking.

The concept of content marketing for a method of building links is easy. All you need to do is make sure your content hits the park and ensure that you're creating current, reliable content in your field. We've talked about the subject in detail and now you have everything you require to write amazing content.

If you write great authentic pieces of content that are reputable, other players in the industry will be drawn with your content. It is able to create hundreds of links. Think about more than 200 backlinks dependent on the niche you are in.

Imagine it in this approach.

This guide has pointed you to various resources can be helpful to you as an affiliate marketer who earns an ongoing passive income. In the same way, if you create excellent content and then share it, other businesses in your industry will link to you in a context as they try to enhance people's lives by enhancing the experience of their viewers.

If your site's niche isn't particularly well-known or seasoned in your particular niche the most effective way to go about it is make the most appealing content you can--highly specific and informative content. You can then begin an outreach campaign that we'll discuss.

A well-written content will naturally draw backlinks from industry experts who believe that linking to your site could provide benefits for their customers. In the past when you are a relatively new site in the niche which is trying to establish its position as the primary authority in the field it is essential to go beyond producing amazing content and be involved with us in outreach.

Outreach is a term used in online marketing to reach out to leaders in the industry who could benefit from the information that you've put together. After you've informed them of your publication, they'll examine it and if it is in line with what they're trying to accomplish with their target customers, they will provide you backlinks in a context.

For this method to implement this strategy,

first think about the type of content you would like to utilize for this method. For example, would the use of a video or an audio source be more effective than a guide or infographic? Deciding on the most effective type of content for your needs is crucial, since various leaders in your niche are drawn to different kinds of content, and since different types of audiences are able to absorb content in different ways.

After you have created your amazing work of art, must then compile your list of top industry figures or businesses in your area and then make contact with these people or businesses to let them know about the most outstanding material or resource.

It is imperative to record something important.

When you approach businesses/individuals you have never interacted with before with the offer to share your content with their audience or a request to link back to your content or page, the said business or individual is likely to overlook your request or give you a negative response. To achieve the best results, make sure you are strategic.

A way to think strategically in this regard is to interact with the person via social media or through the site that is relevant to him or her. Make comments on posts of the person and sign up for the newsletter of his or hers, connect via email or any other method which allows you to establish an intimate connection. If it's done, and you produce great content, and then contact the person asking to share the content with their audience The webmaster is more likely to do it because you've proved yourself an important contributor.

Skyscraper Technique

Skyscraper link building technique Skyscraper link building method was the idea by Brain Dean, the owner of Backlinko. The strategy is so efficient in constructing links and increasing traffic that , when Brian employed the technique, his traffic increased by 106.9 percent. It is a three-step process:

Step 1

First, locate an established linkable asset an expression Brian Dean uses to mean the most popular content in your field. If we take the vegan model we've in this book, that would involve finding amazing pieces of vegan-friendly content and weight loss, which can be done by typing our niche's main keyword in Google Search.

Step 2

In the next step the second step, you design an article that is that is so unique and valuable that it surpasses the established linkable assets you came across on the SERP page for the keywords you intend to use. Be aware that the goal isn't to repeat the identical information. The aim is to create a piece content that in your perspective appears fresh unique, original and superior to previously published content.

For instance, if prior pieces of content you wrote were too complicated, you could write the content with a clear and simple mind. You can write in a manner that makes complex topics easy to comprehend and digest even for non-professionals. It is also possible the option of adding personality or character to the subject or incorporate multimedia to make your article and opinions more attractive. The main idea here is to make content that is superior to all other elements of a linkable asset.

Step 3.

After you have your bit of linkable content that is proven You must be more than merely hoping that Google recognizes the quality of your material, crawls it and instantly gives it the first-page ranking for your keywords of choice. Third step about outreach and marketing.

When you send out emails you make an influencer list that includes those who are likely your informative content and send it to their followers. For the best results, make sure that you inform the influencers you reach out to that they can share the content you have created with your followers they can help them reach their goals of aiding their readers.

Outreach isn't about sending random emails to individuals. The contacts you make with must be other websites and online businesses within your industry , so that, in the end the links you are sent are relevant and connected to the keywords you're aiming for.

Broken Links Strategy

Broken links are another effective strategy for building links. This strategy is very effective as, unlike other strategies we've talked about It does not rely on you to seek links from authoritative sites or webmasters that might not be keen on it.

For implementing this highly effective and simple link building strategy, follow these things:

Step 1

Install Google Chrome and install a broken link checker extension add-on or add-on. LinkMiner immediately is in your thoughts. https://linkminer.com/ https://www.shoutmeloud.com/broken-link-checker-websites.html

LinkMiner along with other tools mentioned on the resource page can help you identify broken links within a webpage.

After installing LinkMiner Once you have installed LinkMiner, make use of Google search to locate pages that have plenty of outbound links i.e. look for a niche-related website or content, which is relevant to the keywords that you wish to optimize for and has links to other pages.

Spend a little time looking for these sites, because you'll notice that websites that have links with external sites, i.e. sites with an active outbound link profile - resource pages are a prime example. They often contain a lot number of damaged links.

The search for resources within your area of expertise is easy when you utilize the following search strings:

"Your keyword" + inurl: links

"Your keyword" + "helpful resources"

"Your keyword" + "useful resources"

"Your keyword" + "useful links"

Once you've found these pages, find a few of them and run the tool to check for broken links you're using on the site or content. If it shows broken links, you should contact your webmaster, or the blogger. Inform them about the links that are broken, and then offer your valuable content to be a replacement for one of the broken links.

Brian Dean recommends using the following script. Remember to modify the script:

Resource Page Strategy

Pages on resource pages provide links to important content. Because resource pages usually contain a lot of outbound links, they're great places to look for links. This strategy for building links is like the other strategies we've discussed, in that it requires you to search for keywords to locate search results that are relevant to your field:

"Your keyword" + inurl:links

"Your keyword" + "helpful resources"

"Your keyword" + "useful resources"

"Your keyword" + "useful links"

When a Google searches return results after which you go through every page and the hyperlinks it has to determine if the fact that a page is linking to you is harmful or beneficial for your site or your backlink profile.

Remember that the goal is to get backlinks from authoritative or niche websites that have high authority in domains and a high rating for URLs.

Also, make sure that your content, including

the one you provide for inclusion on the page of resources, is of high quality. By doing this, it will be easy for Webmasters respond"Yes.
To contact the webmaster who manages the resource page, follow the following script as suggested from Brian Dean:

If you apply these link-building as well as other off-page SEO methods with enthusiasm and with a mindset of growth the traffic you receive will grow and your rank will improve gradually until, eventually you will be at the top of SERPs for the keywords you are looking for.

Steps to Take

Choose the link building and off-page SEO method you'll need to implement first , and then begin the process of implementing it. Be aware that the goal of building links is to ensure that they appear as organic as is possible, meaning that they are contextual links so that Google will consider your niche-related pages and content to be useful and relevant to their intended users.

It is possible to enhance your off-page SEO expertise and build links with the information you can get from the pages below on resources from the industry's top search engine watch as well as Neil Patel, someone who has been mentioned earlier is a pioneer on the SEO and online marketing business.

P.S. Neil Patel's blog is packed with useful information that will be useful as you develop your affiliate marketing company:

In the current stage of your affiliate marketing journey, you've been able to get into the rhythm and your website should be receiving a steady flow of visitors from viewers who are deeply fascinated by the subject that you discuss in blogs.

## Chapter 8: The Way To Do Affiliate Marketing On Facebook

Although most people go straight to their blogs when they are ready to engage in affiliate marketing but there are other methods to reach many more people and earn revenue through your hyperlinks. One method we're going to explore this moment is affiliate marketing via Facebook.

Facebook is among the largest social media platforms with millions of users and billions of accounts use the site every day all over the world. That means you have the possibility of reaching millions of people via your posts, so long as you ensure that you're doing it in the right manner.

Before we begin using Facebook to promote affiliate links, you'll have to create the profile you wish to use. You may choose to use your private profile or decide to create an official profile, depending on the way you wish to run your business. It is important to ensure that the profile begins to showcase your brand,

and only publish content on your page, especially when it's your personal profile, and that line with the business and brand you're trying to build on.

Direct Facebook Traffic onto Your Partner Page

Since the majority of people have their personal Facebook accounts and know how to open new accounts and a new one, it's time to begin the work. You can use your Facebook fans to build up a list of engaging likes until you've got plenty of followers. But if you're employed as an affiliate marketer you can't expect this to assist you until you're able to increase the amount of traffic to go to your page for marketing, and they can make a purchase.

The best method to consider this is as a kind of flirting that can help you develop the relationships you desire instead of going through all guns raised and sending out lots of junk mail. Consider it this way Would you rather give a hand or glance at an article from a close friend who has shown you the product and even spoke to you on occasion , without trying to sell yousomething? Or , would you prefer to have your inbox and website stuffed with messages and spam about the product on a regular basis? Your potential customers are likely be feeling exactly the exact same as you do.

The ideal ratio to consider is 80 percent content that is enjoyable and does not have anything to do with selling (or at the very least, a small amount of selling in the content) and 20 percent for promotion. This will help you develop a strong relationship with potential customers without causing them to feel annoyed and turning people off from visiting your site.

In order for Facebook advertising to benefit your affiliate marketing campaign, you must make sure that your prospective customers truly like your page by using 80 percent of relevant and engaging media. This way that when you make a post with a specific message that are targeted, they'll be more likely to have a look and perhaps even think about purchasing the product.

One thing you must consider is to ensure that the product you are promoting is an affiliate website instead of the direct sale. It is wiser to redirect your traffic into prospects who are familiar with the website you're promoting instead of trying to make more users to your site whether it's an article on your blog, or a special offer for the site's visitors.

When you've managed to attract new customers by providing an appealing reason to return to your website, specifically those who were already on your site at first and then you can send them back to your main site or to the landing page and possibly even add them to your mailing list. This is likely aid in expanding your strategy for affiliate marketing , which is not limited to Facebook and your usual affiliate website. If you're successful in building the list of email addresses you already have, you'll be able to attract customers who are very likely to buy with you in the near future.

Another strategy you could explore is to not only focus on those who already have your profile or page but also try to capture some of the vast audience active on Facebook and have them sent to your affiliate website. Facebook Ads is among the most effective ways to achieve this. There are a variety of choices you can work with to get Facebook Ads, including pay-per-click advertising and the pay per 1,000 impressions. You can test these options to find out which will be the most effective for your requirements. Facebook Ads can help you reach the best target audience because Facebook provides information that will enhance your advertising campaigns. You can search for details about the user's age and their location, the place they are employed, their preferences are, and much more. This is beneficial because you can target precisely the people you wish to target and drive visitors to one of the affiliate's products more quickly than previously.

Making an advertisement for your business on Facebook is quite simple. You can log into your personal account or business account and choose the drop-down menu under settings page or by using the small wheel in the upper right-hand corner of your page. It is likely that you will discover a wide range of options which are designed to meet various objectives. If you're looking to ensure that more people visit your site and be engaged and involved in conversation, then select the most effective option. For page likes then you'd choose this option. To direct those customers or members of the audience to your affiliate site, you could try website conversions to determine how many clicks are happening and convert to the sign-ups you need as per the strategy.

If you're looking to make use of this marketing campaign to attract people to sign up for your offers or content, use the Clicks On Website. You can then browse through and include your site and some images to accompany it. You must include more than one picture in order to really attract your clients, but six is the number you should strive for. keep to the size that is recommended for images that measure around 300 per 315 pixels.

The other thing you can do is linking the new advertisement to the Facebook page. The link will take your visitors to your site after clicking it, however this can help you gain some extra exposure as well as it will create hyperlinks and connections between your website and the Facebook page. It is also possible to consider including an action button for a simpler experience.

## Chapter 9: Email Marketing

Marketing via email is among the most effective strategies for digital marketing. Many studies have shown that email marketing is more successful than other kind of advertising. If you've got your own email database, you can communicate with your leads in a an immediate way, develop them, and eventually convert your leads into loyal clients.

Email is the top communication channel. A majority of consumers across the globe make use of mail as the main channel of communication. Most of them must check at their email each day. This is why email marketing is the most effective marketing methods. Because email marketing can be profitable, to some degree, it is contingent on the ability to target. You should collect the emails from people who you are certain will be interested in your item and have buying power. For instance, if your site is operating a site that teaches people to camp, you'll want to reach out to not just those who are attracted to camping, but also those who are willing to spend money to purchase the products you're selling.

Your email list belongs to you.

Another reason that marketing via email is so effective is because you control the list. If you consider all the other platforms affiliate marketers can use for example Facebook twitter, LinkedIn, or Instagram You must realize that you could end up being banned. If you are banned from these platforms , it implies that you've lost your followers which can seriously impact your income. If you've got an email address, it's always yours. You'll always have possibility of contacting these individuals and you can continue advertising to them. The majority of people who earn large sums of money through online marketing have a huge email list.

Buyers of email are more expensive

Many studies have shown that people who are offered emails from their list are more likely to purchase fourteen times more often than those who purchase through other methods. Also, you must realize that when you've got an email list that is responsive that you could get a client to buy multiple times over the course of a single purchase, unlike the case of a banner that is only once and then the sale is over. Email marketing gives the opportunity to present your product more clearly and more effectively, something that is not possible about banners or using any other marketing strategy.

Lead magnets

The internet's most successful marketers realize that there is no free lunch. This is why you don't find them saying, give me your email just in the name of it. They've mastered their art at attracting leads. They achieve this through the using lead magnets. Lead magnets are essentially the equivalent of a bargaining chip. A marketer on the internet might ask you to provide your email address so that they can email you an crucial resource you'll need. A few of the most sought-after lead magnets Internet marketers use include eBooks and resource lists case studies including free trials, webinars, free consultations, coupons.

However, you must be aware that just because you have an email list does not mean anything. It is essential to do the work to generate the sales. Here are a few actions you need to take to increase the value from your list of email subscribers.

* Know your audience

Don't be the marketer who simply blasts his customers with ever-changing emails without knowing who they are and what they are looking for. If you really wish to know your customers then you should ask for their feedbackand must always encourage them leave comments on your different platforms. You might also wish to conduct surveys with your followers. Send them an email and request them to take part with your poll.

* Send out regular emails

Every successful affiliate marketer has one thing they all have in common: they've learned their art of promotion via emails. They realize that they shouldn't send out one email only to sit for weeks before sending another one. Allow your readers to become accustomed to your. Set up a schedule to send emails. Don't be the lazy kind of person who just sends out one email repeatedly. Develop your creative skills and try your hand at words and make your subscribers laugh. You aren't looking to be perceived as being too busy.

* Write a powerful subject line
If you're having trouble getting open rates One of the reasons might be that your voice sounds like an automated machine. People will pay attention to your personality if you make it sound like fun. You don't have to be a shrewd person to do it. A well-written subject line ensures that your reader will take a look and say wow! Always improve yourself by studying books, magazines and newspapers, as it will provide you with new ideas and help you develop an out-of-the-box thinking.

* Keep your email so short
When people check the emails you send them, you do not want to create the impression that they're reading a book. Be sure to make use of vivid language to convey the essence of what you are trying to convey.

Even though we're saying your emails need to be brief and concise, they should nevertheless contain the essential tenets of what you're trying to promote. Keep in mind that omitting any pertinent information from buyers is a type of fraud. Do not let your customers feel like they've been cheated since they'll be furious and will most likely not subscribe. If your customers feel treated with respect, they'll become loyal customers.

* Don't shout

The people you are writing to have a strong support for your company The most that you could do is to show them respect. If you write using capital letters you're definitely not showing anyone any respect. Use normal language and a normal format. This will let your customers know that you're well-informed and considerate.

• Learn how to settle conflicts

at the conclusion of our day, we're mere mortals. If you're handling an extensive mailing list of subscribers, you may be lucky enough to deal with a crazed person or group of crazy people. If you're not able to handle an emergency, you could be tempted to send an angry email to all your subscribers. This could affect your relationship with them. Keep in mind that your online customers don't owe anything to you or feel that they are not treated with respect in any way it is possible that they will choose to unsubscribe. If you meet people who are unhappy with the way you run your business, you should first of all , give them some focus to determine whether there's any truth to it. However, should you discover that they're driven by pure malice and jealousy issue, you should eliminate them.

* Don't send offers every time.

Don't become the frustrated affiliate marketer constantly bombarding his followers with promotions. Give your customers some reason to consider, something that will keep them entertained, or something to think about. This is an extremely effective marketing strategy because it's an opportunity to let your subscribers think of the company. Don't let the illusion fool you, humans are people, and every one of us is curious about what we can gain from others. Therefore, if you're the person who provides worth to others, you'll be held with respect.

## Chapter 10: Selecting The Right Domain Name (Expired Vs. Fresh And Emd Vs. Pmd)

The process of choosing a domain isn't given as much importance in the process of building any affiliate niche website.

A debate that has been going on for quite a long time in relation to deciding on a domain name is

Which is better: Expired Domain or a New Domain? The one I picked for my website had an expiring domain which helped me gain an edge in the ranking of the articles.

There are many things you must be aware of if you're choosing to take the path of expired domains:

The greatest benefit of having an expired domain is that you already have multiple websites that are linked to your domain which can provide lots of potential to rank your site quickly.

I would however advise you to be cautious about going the in the expired domain route, as the most desirable domains sell at $100's, and only the

The spammy ones are accessible for sale at a low cost.

Now , you might wonder what's so great do you think of Fresh domains?

Buying fresh domains is like buying a brand new car. You know that you'll be first owner of it and there will be no other parties in the process.

This can be helpful if you're novice and don't want to burn yourself while selecting an old domain.

Even with a brand new domain, you will be able to get a good ranking and earn money from your site in a short time (3-4 month).

So don't ponder over expired domains, even if you're unable to locate a suitable one in the next moment... take advantage of the domain again.

After having gone through the steps involved in purchasing domain names we can discuss the process of choosing the domain name.

EMD v/s PMD (Exact Match Domains v/s Partial Match Domain)

Let's say the primary keyword I'm aiming for is the best Gas Grill under 1000

Here's how an Exact Match Domain might look like:bestGasgrill1000.com

It doesn't take a genius of a brain to recognize the ugly look of EMD... extremely ugly.

There was an era in SEO that you could rank quickly with the EMD domain... however, the days of EMD domains are over for good.

Today, it is all about creating an authority, and about creating an image and if your website looks awful, your site is bound to be a major snare.

Partially Match Domain (PMD) on the other hand are more effective versions of EMD's.

you are able to only use one principal word or A synonym for that word is the domain of yours.

So, if the phrase I'm aiming for would be Best Gas Grill under 1000 the domain I choose

It could be: GasGrill.com or SmokyGasGrill.com instead.

(I recognize that the domain names are funny, but I'm unable to think of good names in a hurry.)

It allows me to create an identity that is simple that is easily brandable, and allows users to type directly the name directly into browsers.

If you follow this crucial guide, you'll surely create a unique and memorable domain name.

"The goal here is to strike a appropriate balance between picking an appropriate domain that is easily brandable, regardless of whether you're picking a brand new domain or taking the route of expired domains."

Hosting and Site Setup

With a well-studied area and a domain with a stunning design You now require a web hosting provider that is capable of handling your website effectively.

What type of hosting do you need?

Based on your technical abilities You have two choices when choosing a hosting plan for your site of interest. Choose either Shared Hosting as well as Cloud VPS plans.

For shared hosting, I highly suggest using Namechep.com or digitalocean.com since they provide one of the most reliable hosting services available that I've seen.

DigitalOcean is the most reliable in cloud VPS hosting. (Not advised if you're just beginning your journey)

But I've already published an in-depth guide for setting up an WordPress website on DigitalOcean.

There's always a huge debate over whether you should go with Cloud VPS or Shared Hosting hosting, but I'd recommend deciding on your experience.

If you're just beginning, Shared Hosting happens to be the most effective alternative... however, you're aware of the issues you're experiencing when using Shared Hosting opting for the VPS option could be an alternative.

Making a decision on the theme and setting your Website:

I can't count the number of times I've been acknowledged by fellow bloggers for the theme and design I picked for my niche blog. A theme selection isn't just about aesthetics or fancy components. It's all about loading speed and an effective SEO optimization.

It doesn't mean that you have to pick one that is boring and appears to be from into 2000.To get straight to the main point, a theme that I strongly suggest would be Schema from themeforest.net because, not only can customize the theme to your preference, but it's SEO optimized, with a speedy loading speed and Schema markup, which can give you an edge to your competition.

If you're not a fan of the Schema theme themes, those from developers such as Thrive Themes and Studiopress happens to be worthy of a mention.

The most important things to think about when making your Wordpress website:

Install WP on root domain itself and not on 'yourdomian.com/blog'. A lot of times we do not take note of this and it's not the best method to accomplish it.

Choose the primary and secondary colors for your site: The primary color is generally the color that will be the basis of your website and is used in the logo, navigation bar, popups, footer and more...

After you have installed the theme, you can write a test article and test various colors that go well. Check that you have the primary colors and secondary colours must be in contrast to one primary colors and secondary colors should be in contrast to each. You can use Adobe Kuler to finalize a color scheme for your website.

Here's a list of the top 5 blogs and their HEX color code they use for its primary colors.

Buzzfeed.com - #e32

Techcrunch.com - #089e00

Mashable.com - #00aeef

Neilpatel.com - #f16334

Hongkiat.com - #26519e

Make sure that your site doesn't appear like any other site you are competing with. In the present day where people are occupied with numerous things, it's just the things they see that they remember.

If your website looks as your competition's... you're an unproductive opportunity to create a change.

The majority of niche websites ignore this vital aspect, which can help us present ourselves more effectively. To help you get inspired, apply the color scheme or style of any authoritative site which is not connected to your specific niche.

For my personal website for my own site, I (shamelessly) used a color schemes from a prominent SEO/Blogging site. I refer to this as the "Parasite Color' strategy, in which you use the aspects of the design of an established website, but not relevant to your particular niche.

Like the colors, you should use two fonts for your website . One font to be used to represent content, and another font that represents headings, the Nav Font, Logo, Sidebar and other things. In today's world I strongly recommend selecting only Sans-serif fonts that aren't overly thin or robust, and can be easy to read on desktops and mobile screens.

Here's a list of the most popular Sans Serif font: 1. Lato

2. Open Sans

3. Montserrat

4. Source Sans Pro

5. Raleway

Be sure to check how your website appears on tablets and mobiles while you edit its look and feel on your desktop. I didn't pay attention to this aspect and my previous site had problems with mobile rendering and appeared ugly. Utilize the Google Mobile Friendly Tool to test the your mobile friendly site and make any necessary adjustments as is suggested from the software.

# Chapter 11: Affiliate Passive Income From Blogging

The term "blog" refers to a page or site that conveys any thought or idea and is updated regularly by the admin or the owner. It is usually run by a person who has specific ideas or an individual or a group with an objective. It usually will be written in a relaxed way using a conversational tone or in a casual manner. If you enjoy keeping a journal and would like to share it on the internet with a larger amount of people it is likely that you are using blogs to share your thoughts with the world and to share your thoughts on any topic. A blog is therefore an individual journal that is regularly updated frequently and is posted online. In short, a blog, a weblog is an display of your thoughts and thoughts.

Why do we blog?

Another question that pops to our attention is why you require on your own site. The answer is quite straightforward. Everyone has a right to speak and be heard by other. Written material and books require investment and a lot of work. Printing your work is a difficult task which requires energy, time and, of course, money. Consequently, the market you want to target will be restricted. If you have your own blog, you'll be able to publish your thoughts on the internet, and can spread your message to all of the world. You'll meet like-minded people who share the same viewpoint on the subject or issue you are interested in. In less time and without cost, your message will reach hundreds of thousands of people. It is the responsibility of the blogger to write and share the details of their daily life with their followers. There are a variety of bloggers who write about their lives eating, how they eat, and the joys of life. there's also a class of bloggers who run their blogs on a particular topic they are passionate about. Numerous blogs covering a variety of topics provide examples for the diversity of topics that bloggers can blog about.

The internet blogs offer information on celebrities from various kinds of lives including beauty tips, politics as well as the current news at a both the international and national level investment, games and sports, conflicts and wars around the globe natural disasters, technological knowledge and other home-related topics such as gardening, cooking interior design kitchen equipment, laundry machines and more. They also provide tips on how to use blog to educate the viewers. Personal blogs are also very popular with readers, and businesses also utilize blogs to market their products as well as keep in contact with their customers.

Earning money from your blog

This chapter will show you how to make your blog profitable. It will give you strategies, tips and strategies that you can employ to begin earning income from your brand new blog.

The Techniques

CPC (i.e. Cost per Click) Ads

Many bloggers make money from their websites with Cost Per Click ads. Like the name implies it is the CPC advertiser pays you every time a visitor clicks an ad. Adsense is among Google's advertising services, is the most well-known CPC alternative today. Through Adsense Google is going to check the content of your documents. It will then search for ads that are relevant to the content. Since the ads are connected to the blog entries themselves This advertising method yields excellent results.

Important Note: You'll be able to learn more about Adsense in the following chapter.

This program offers a variety of benefits for bloggers as well as readers. It allows bloggers to earn income from their articles. It also helps readers to find the products and/or services they want.

CPM (i.e. Cost per Thousand) Ads

This type of advertising system is paid based on the number of people who are exposed to the advertisements. CPM stands for "Click-to-Meal" and the "M" on the CPM is the Roman numeral , which represents 1,000. There isn't much to earn from this advertising system in the initial few months during the beginning of blogging. But, when your blog receives a significant amount of visitors, CPM can help

you make huge amounts of cash. These are the most well-known CPM websites currently:
* Adbrite.com
* Pulsepoint.com
* Casalemedia.com
* AdClickMedia.com
* Technoratimedia.com
* Adify.com

Each one of these networks have distinct advantages and disadvantages. It is best if you study each one prior to putting them to your blog. This way, you'll be able to ensure you're using a CPM system you're adopting meets your requirements.

Affiliate Products

As blogger, you are able to be an intermediary between potential buyers and sellers. You can make partnerships with individuals or companies who provide products or services associated with your blog. You will then promote these products or services in blogs posts. This way you make money every time someone in your audience pays for the products or services you recommend.

This system of advertising transforms you into an salesperson. In contrast to conventional salespeople, you can advertise products or services to thousands of customers and make alliances with a variety of sellers.

Here are the most effective affiliate programs you can apply to your website:

* Flexoffers.com
* LinkShare.com
* Shareasale.com
* CJ.com
* E-Junkie.com
* Affiliate-program.amazon.com
* Panthera.com
* LogicalMedia.com
* RedPlum.com
* MoneySavingMom.com
* Coupons.com
* MySavings.com

It is best if you're sincere with all of your suggestions. Provide an honest opinion on the items and/or services that you feature through your site. For example, you can write an article that outlines the advantages and disadvantages of a product in order to inform your readers on the benefits of that offering. The system is effective because it serves three parties at once. Earn money from your referrals. Sellers gain more customers. Your readers, on other hand, are educated about the products and services they might require. The details about affiliate advertising in the future.

Ad Space

There is also the option to give advertising space to online marketing companies. Many bloggers have tried this method and have succeeded. Advertising space to advertisers is extremely effective in specific niche markets. To implement this advertising system on your blog, go to www.buysellads.com. www.buysellads.com website. The site helps bloggers and marketers connect.

The Timeframe

If you've learned how to make money from your blog It is likely that you would like to know how long it will take to make a steady flow of money. It's crucial to remember that blogging isn't the fastest method to earn money. It requires a lengthy time frame. Even the most successful bloggers had to be patient for months (or perhaps years) to earn an adequate amount of money.

It is obvious that you can reduce the duration significantly if you are already familiar with topics such as advertising writing, the creation of content and search engine optimization and other subjects related to blogging.

How to Make the Most of Adsense

The second section of the book will teach you sophisticated techniques. These strategies are intended to increase the amount you earn via the Google Adsense program. When you apply these strategies to your site, you will be able to increase by a factor of two (or perhaps triple) the amount you earn from Adsense.

It is important to note that every blog is different. Even blogs belonging to the same niche may differ in layout and readers as well as articles. These factors greatly impact the your potential earnings through using the

Adsense program. But, the strategies listed below can assist you in your Adsense campaign, regardless of your subject matter, layout and the current blog entries.

1. Advertisements should be placed in places that draw eye of your readers. Remember that you earn money through Adsense every time a visitor is able to click on the advertisements. This means that you must place the ads in most attractive areas on your website. However, you must also be mindful of the overall user-friendliness of your website. If you place Adsense advertisements with reckless abandon the readers may stop coming to your site. To reap the maximum benefit from Adsense you have be able to understand the process of placement.

2. You can target specific sections of your blog posts - By using this method, you can pinpoint the specific parts of your blog entries that Google will consider when selecting ads. Implementing this method on your blog is straightforward and straightforward. You just have to type."

Affiliate marketing In the next section we will discuss the benefits of promoting with partners. It is crucial to explore and find out your opportunities in your chosen specialization prior to launching your blog. For those who don't have a idea of what the partner's business is, it's the area where you can offer an article on your site that has an affiliation that is only interesting to the visitors of your site. If someone decides to buy that item through your site you'll get an amount of commission.

Offshoot marketing is the method that the majority of, if not all bloggers make money So don't be apathetic about this method of earning money. The best way to check if your site has the appropriate offshoot plan is to go to Amazon.com and look through each of the products that can be purchased based on the subject you are interested in. If they have plenty of merchandise available to market, at that moment you've found the right one. In the next section, we'll talk about other options related to partner-based marketing, but currently, do not do not worry about Amazon and the products they offer.

Monetizing

The act of monetizing your blog website means that you are allowing Google to display advertisements on your blog. When people click on the advert, you'll make the money. The best way to find out if your field is getting a large quantity of Google marketing and advertising is to just search for your "search term."

If your focus is yoga exercises, Google yoga exercise in the search bar. The more ads that you come across related to your specific area, the better chance you'll be able to earn revenue from the monetization of your blog website. Earning money from your blog is a great way to earn even more money through your blog especially if you've got many users who visit your blog.

Final research

In order to get an understanding of your subject, you have to log onto "Google Patterns." This is where you'll surely discover how regular your subject is as well as the amount of people are actively looking for content on your subject. All you have to do is type in your search term into the web search engine and it will provide you with a graph. Make sure you're looking at a chart that includes at minimum five years of data. If your chart remains within the middle to high level while remaining consistent while at the same time, then you've chosen the appropriate topic. If, however, your chart is slowly decreasing year on year, then it's the right time to choose a fresh blog topic.

If you meet all the requirements listed above, at, then you've got the right subject matter and you are able to start your blog whenever you can. If not you're in, then I'd like you to reconsider your subject and come up with an entirely new one that does fulfill all the requirements listed above.

However, you must make sure that you earn money from your blog and not just writing for it. Continue to browse and keep looking as long as you'll find your ideal topic. I'm sure you'll be able to identify your subject in a

couple of photos.
Benefits of Utilizing WordPress

It is vital to create your blog. There are a lot of Wordpress.com technical guides available to help you with the creation of your blog, but they are not specifically designed to help you improve your blog on the perspective of marketing. However, if your blog's content is not optimized from a marketing perspective it is not going to stand the greatest chance of retaining visitors and turning them into buyers. It is important to think about the marketing potential of your website. In this section we will help you optimize your blog so that your readers are not just captivated by your blog the very first time they come there, but are enticed to follow your blog, bookmark you and search for your blog on other platforms so that they are up-to-date on your blog's content and the wonderful content you post.

Your Template

The first step in creating a successful, marketable blog is ensuring that you're using the correct template. On Wordpress you will find many templates to pick from. If you are unable to discover what you are looking for on their site or blog, you can perform an Google search and discover other third-party businesses that create Wordpress templates which you can download and add onto your website.

Finally, you must select a template that is mobile-friendly. The majority of your visitors will be reading your content on their phones. The majority of users access your website from desktops, so although you should ensure that your website is compatible with desktops and also, making your website mobile-friendly is essential. Websites that aren't designed for mobile use are swiftly discarded in favor of those that are. Be sure to look at the appearance of your template on mobile devices, and make sure that all the features are functional and easy to read and simple to read, to ensure that readers appreciate your blog.

## Chapter 12: What Happens If You Decide To Add Ppc In Your Affiliate Programs?

PPC typically come with ready-to-use tools for affiliates that can be easily integrated into your site. The most commonly used tools are search boxes banners, text links , and some 404 error pages. The majority of search engines use specific solutions, and could offer an affiliate program that is white-label. This allows you, with just a few pages of code to incorporate the co-branded, remote-hosted program on your site.

The most important advantages? It's not just extra cash but also some additional cash in the form of a side income. Also, an ongoing commission after you've added a few webmaster friends to join the engine.

Take a look. How can you earn these benefits , while already earning some revenue for your site? Understanding a few of the most useful tools to use in the affiliate program will not be an unnecessary time-waster. They're a means of earning while earning.

Learn more about how you'll incorporate PPC search engines in your affiliate program, rather than missing out on a great opportunity to increase your profits.

Utilizing Product Recommendations for extending Your Bottom Line

When it comes to Affiliate marketing, you can find a few methods that can help you earn more money and keep the account you have worked so hard to earn already. A majority of the strategies and strategies are mastered quickly. You don't have to leave or wait for a long time. They're online 24/7, all week long.

One of the most important methods of increasing affiliate marketing's sales and profits is to make use of product suggestions. Many marketers are aware that this is of the most efficient methods of promoting a certain product.

If visitors or buyers are confident in you, they'll be able to be able to trust your recommendations. Be cautious when using this method, however. If you start promoting anything based on recommendations then your credibility will be damaged. This happens most often when the recommendations seem exaggerated and have no merit.

Don't be afraid to talk about things that you do not like about certain items or products. Instead of losing points it can increase the credibility of your recommendations and may increase your credibility.

Additionally, if the people who visit your site are truly interested in the products you offer they'll be thrilled to discover what's great about the product, the negatives and how it will benefit them.

If you're going to recommend the use of a specific product There are a few points to remember about how to use it efficiently and to your benefit. You sound like the real and most renowned expert in your area.

Take note of this simple equation: price resistance decreases in directly proportion to confidence. If your clients believe and trust that you're knowledgeable in your field and they're more likely to purchase that product. But when you're not displaying confidence or self-assurance when affirming your services and services, they'll likely think the same and will search for a different product or service that seems more credible.

How can one create this level of expertise? by offering unique and innovative solutions that people can't find elsewhere. Make sure that what you're advertising works as you stated. Include prominent testimonials and endorsements of reputable and well-known personalities within related areas.

When recommending a product it's important to offer promotional giveaways. Many people are already familiar with the idea of giving away giveaways to promote your own product. However, only a handful of people use it to promote affiliate products. Offer freebies that could promote or even contain details about your product or services.

Before you include recommendations to the product you're selling, just as important to try to test the product and offer support. Don't risk advertising products that aren't worth your time.

Commissions Overnight

The ideal scenario for affiliate marketing doesn't need your own website, managing customers as well as refunds, development, and maintenance. This is typically one of the easiest methods of starting an online business, and earning more money.

If you're already in some kind of affiliate programme, what's the next thing you'd like to accomplish? Perhaps triple, or double your commissions, surely? What is the best way to do this?

Here are some effective suggestions for how to increase the commissions you earn from affiliate programs in a matter of minutes.

Find the easiest product and program to sell. You'd like to sell the program that allows you to earn the highest returns in the shortest time.

There are many aspects to take into consideration when selecting this kind of program. Select programs that offer an extensive commission structure. Are they products that fit with your customers. That includes a solid calendar of easy payment to their affiliate and punctually. If you are unable to make your investment grow then you should get rid of the program and continue to find a better one.

There are a myriad of affiliate programs available online that provide an opportunity to pick your favorite. You should pick the most straightforward to ensure you don't lose any advertising funds.

Create free reports or brief E-Books to share via your site. There's a high probability that you're competing against other affiliates who offer similar programs. If you start writing an article that is brief and focuses on the product you're selling then you'll have the ability to stand out from other affiliates.

In the reports, include important information no cost. If you are able, add suggestions about the product. With E-Books, you get credibility. Your customers will notice this in you and will be drawn to take advantage of the services you offer.

2. Save and collect the email addresses of the people who download Your free E-Books.

It's a proven fact that nobody makes sales on

their first invitation. You'll need to make your message six times in order to create an order. This is the primary reason you should keep track of the contact details of the people customers who purchased your documents as well as E-Books. Follow-ups will be sent to the contacts to remind them to make a purchase from you.

## Chapter 13: Tips You Must To Know About Success In Affiliate Marketing

If done correctly, affiliate marketing can provide you with a substantial income stream. Many people don't consider how their actions impact their performance or failure to take action. Therefore, let's review 6 various tips you should be aware of to ensure that you're successful in affiliate marketing.

#1 Don't open your email more often than two times a day

Did you consider that email is among the most frequent interruption that people have to deal with every day. Instead of checking your email every couple of minutes or once an hour, why don't you check your email once in the middle of the day, and again at night. You can check it out, and then to focusing on the things to be done. The less often you check your email, the more efficient you'll become and the more effective your affiliate marketing could be.

#2 Say 'no' and then say it.

Many of us find that saying no is nearly impossible. But, if you wish to be on track and experience success in affiliate marketing you will need to be able to say no. This will help you keep your attention from being interrupted constantly. It may also assist in not take on too many things.

#3 Do the job that is the worst first.

If you do the most difficult task first then it's accomplished and you're ready to proceed with your life. It's easy to put off doing something because it's something you do not wish to do. It keeps your mind busy and you'll be unable to catch up because you're doing nothing.

## Chapter 14: Myths About Affiliate Marketing

Myth of Affiliate Marketing: It's really easy
Truth: You'll find numerous people who claim that affiliate advertising is the easiest method of establishing an online business. If you think about it, all it's all you need is an effective website as well as affiliate link to set your business. Although it may seem easy to achieve, the reality is that it's not as easy as you imagine. Like any other type of business it requires funds and time to get it to be successful. Absolutely not, just having a website and affiliate marketers it is likely to be successful right away. The most difficult thing to those working in this specific field is creating a website.

You must have the right information that your customers require and also information that's good enough to draw more people. It is also essential to design keywords and utilize the most effective Seo methods to make sure you're proficient in obtaining Positive Many

Meanings , or good rankings. Also, you need resources available e.g. videos, links and written content that will allow you to create the creation of your own website.

Additionally but you need to be proficient in promoting your content and materials you've created to social media. Each of these is required if you'd be successful and make money from affiliate marketing.

Myth: A lot of visitors also mean the possibility of earning a lot of money

Based on the facts that show how directing people to the website you own can help you earn an enormous amount of money. It's true that it doesn't require you to have lots of visitors to make a conversion. What benefit does it offer you in the event that you're diverting many visitors to your site but you don't see any conversion? Keep in mind that when any visitors visit the site on your own, the interests of their own could alter and conversion is dependent on the content you provide. This means that you don't require a huge amount of traffic to succeed (although certain, having a large amount of traffic can help) because the revenue is much lower.

The Myth Affiliate marketing is dying

Truth: Many claim that affiliate advertising is utilized however the reality is that it's just evolving and the current pattern is quite different from the time it was first imagined. Trends that are emerging tend to be more restricted , and affiliates are not allowed to engage in advertising with links, while banners are reduced. Google 's algorithms are strict regarding content, as well as SEO strategies and sites which do not meet the requirements are moved to the end of the results page. Banner advertisements are also restricted due to the fact that they're not compatible with smartphones today. The size of the images used are considerably less effective than they were in the past. These days, banners are replaced by single-way links that you can to locate between blogs you stumble across.

Myth: Social media posts you make will be automatically shared and likes

The truth is that social media is an excellent source of marketing at no cost for Affiliate marketing. However, keep also in awareness that nothing on it is free, as there are instances when ads are paid for. But for your posts or content that you create to be shared, or maybe even liked, it is essential that you must publish something that is also interesting. It must be something that can draw people's attention. Writing an article or even curate data (the method to accomplish it) can help, however anything social networking takes time, but if you are aware of what you must do, then you can think of each piece as an asset which will result in a positive returns shipping.

Myth: Only a handful of areas are lucrative

The truth is that it's easy to say that some niches are more lucrative than others, but you must find the most lucrative niche so that you can earn profit. Every niche market is profitable however how you market and also improve your marketing plays a significant aspect in its success. In the end we can affirm that the talents that you have be more significant than the subject you've picked. How do you choose the most suitable area?

Begin by identifying your interests, hobbies or hobbies. What are you most passionate about? Once you've figured out what these are the next steps, it's will be much simpler to promote your business and enhance the market you've got.

Myth: It's all about making commissions and sales alone.

The truth is that the most important aspect of affiliate advertising is to attract new customers as well as the highest amount of traffic. Commissions and sales are a part of the many advantages you can get from this company. The benefits aren't restricted to commissions and sales only because there are numerous tasks that you can perform when dealing in affiliate marketing. There's Seo compliance and guests, landing pages leads, landing pages, and many more to handle.

Myths: Affiliate Marketing can be a decrease in business

The truth is that, as I've said the fact that affiliate advertising is changing the way businesses operate. Contrary to popular belief that affiliate marketing isn't declining, although the fact is that there's a constant increase for businesses that use affiliate programs mainly because customers who are visiting affiliate sites are more likely to spend more money as compared to other clients.

Myth: Contents can be capable of standing on their own by itself Seo as well as affiliate marketing

Truth: Writing content is essential, although content is able to deliver results, the work you do does not stop there. You need to keep producing quality content in order to succeed in marketing. This is the very first step to take when it comes to affiliate marketing. To do this, you must write as well as publish regularly. The use of unique titles and images is capable of attracting readers. The same applies to the addition of videos. In addition to videos and pictures podcasts, sharing links and sharing them via social networks are great methods to promote your content. That's why, content on its own isn't enough; you need to think outside the box and have a variety of ways to promote it.

Affiliate marketing isn't just a stroll through

the woods; in actual fact, you need to be serious about it if you are looking to earn money from it. Now that you know the truth of these myths, make sure that you consider all the factors before you begin to design the plan independently before deciding to jump in the leap. In the end the best plan will be a safe choice is it not?